LIVING WITHOUT HIM

A journey of love, loss and hope

MINERVA KHAJURIA

notionpress.com

INDIA • SINGAPORE • MALAYSIA

ISBN
Paperback 979-8-89544-538-9
Hardcase 979-8-89588-380-8

To Abhinav

To life and beyond, to death and beyond

Contents

Contents

Part IV Living Without Him: My Father

Part V Months After

Part VI Living Without Them

Preface

I am not a storyteller. This is perhaps the only story I will ever tell, because this is the only story I have ever lived.

For all intents and purposes, I am a nobody.

If you ever get to know me, you will find that I am as ordinary as they come. You wouldn't even notice me amidst the vast sea of people in Gurgaon. I look the same as the hundreds of thousands of 30-something corporate dwellers who inhabit the city; who can be found in and around the flourishing office spaces, beaming with pride in their fancy suits, clutching their designer bags and blabbering away on their expensive phones, their confident smiles and sleek hair on point. I am one of them, although my unassured grin may contrast with their confidence, and my untreated frizzy hair may stand out among the sleek hairstyles.

If you and I do cross paths and manage to get acquainted, and one day you end up probing me about my life, my past, my story after you share yours, I will tell you who I am. But I will only share the glossy details of my fabulous job in consulting, my recent international travels and my family that loves me beyond measure. I will speak only of the joys of living, skipping entirely my harrowing encounters with mortality. Because, perhaps, by then, acceptance would have settled in, easing the fury that consumes me to this day.

But you might meet me on other days as well. Days when I am feeling defeated, yet again, by the burden of the past that I carry alone. Days when you might get an entirely different narrative, when I might tell you the story of the two men in my life—my father and my husband—and how those men perished, seven years apart, in my own arms, while I tried desperately to do something, anything, to save them, to save the life that I had hoped to build around them.

I wouldn't tear up when I talk about them, because I would have shed my fair share of tears by then. My stare would be blank, my mind foreseeing your reaction. You would struggle for words, secretly wishing you hadn't asked me that question in the first place. Watching you fumble like that might even bring me a slight sadistic delight, even if only for a moment.

Thereafter, we will continue to be acquaintances, but our conversations will be limited to the more trivial aspects of our current lives: exploring new dining spots, travel plans, pending promotions, weekend trips to the mall, the new iPhone that you recently bought. We would not indulge in the past again. We would cease all discourse on life and its realities from there on.

You see, life and its realities are often stranger than fiction could ever be. Of course, life is brutal, and when it hits you, there is anguish and grief, a fogginess in the brain, and actual tangible, physical pain that accompanies all that trauma. But then, there comes a point when that torment starts to play second fiddle and all you are left with is utter bemusement.

Your life bemuses you, more than you ever thought it had the ability to. You find yourself so baffled by the turn of events that you begin to question your entire existence. You begin to believe that you are nothing but a prisoner of your fate, that whatever you may decide to do, you can never break the shackles and truly lay claim to freedom.

Sure, this state of defencelessness is often interrupted by sporadic glimmers of hope—that one day, in a far and distant future, your fate will take mercy on you and set you free. But soon enough your mind brings you back to a place where you can't even fathom ever seeing that day. You know that you will only be truly free once you cease to exist and your powdery residue vanishes into the elements of earth.

Life has agitated me to the point that I can't contain any of it within me any longer. I feel an intense, urgent need to distil it all into words that I am familiar with and jot it all down. I want to scribble it into clearly legible letters on spotless pieces of paper while it is all still fresh. I want my life to become a tangible account that I could read and reread again, in the hope that all of it will make sense one day.

I want to write it all down so that years later, when life might feel marginally normal again, I don't forget any of it. I don't become less vigilant. I don't trivialise it all into a nightmare that I had now woken up from. That it couldn't have possibly happened before and that it can't possibly happen again.

I can't deny that this account also stems from a lingering desire for validation from absolute strangers that, yes, my life *has* been hard. That if I go insane, my insanity would be perfectly justifiable. Perhaps, deep down, I yearn for my suffering to be seen, to be acknowledged. For I am yet to receive the heart-wrenching response that I have secretly but desperately craved for the last year and a half. I am yet to see the horrors in the eyes of others that I wanted to see, I am yet to see them go speechless with astonishment.

What I have managed to garner so far, is some pity, and that I refuse to accept.

Perhaps I will not receive the validation that I long for; perhaps it wasn't that hard after all. Because all over the world, there are hundreds and thousands of harrowing tragedies unfolding every minute. Perhaps I am just overestimating the weight of my suffering, but I'll let you be the judge of that.

Part I

He Too Left Me

1

He Died

It was 8 am, but already hot and unbearable. The sun was up high, burning down on us in all its glory, making the aridness of the Delhi May morning insufferable. And yet, my body couldn't feel any of it. It felt terribly cold. It could have been exhaustion, or perhaps I was running a fever. I wouldn't really know; I wasn't thinking about any of it.

The centre of all my consciousness was something else. I had just returned from the hospital where Abhinav, my husband of a year, had been admitted for the past fifteen days. It wasn't our home in Gurgaon that I had come back to, which Abhinav and I hadn't visited for a month now. Or Abhinav's parents' house in Delhi, where we had been camping for the last month as the second wave of the COVID-19 pandemic intensified. I had come back to Abhinav's grandmother's house.

This house, a ten-minute drive from the hospital, had become our temporary refuge these past few days. It was the house that Abhinav had spent some of his formative years in. Since our wedding, he had wanted to bring me here; eager to share the memories of his childhood and to introduce me to his chacha and chachi, who still lived in the house. But our plans had been thwarted by the arrival of the COVID-19 outbreak shortly after our wedding.

A deep sense of loneliness enveloped me as I stepped inside Abhinav's childhood home without him by my side.

Abhinav's aunt had very graciously set up a bedroom for me on the first floor where I could rest for a couple of hours before heading back to the hospital. It was only the second time I was meeting her since our wedding. I took a cold shower and slipped into a kurta I had borrowed from her. She also brought me some warm potato sandwiches to eat. Despite not having eaten a morsel for the past eighteen hours, I found my appetite lacking. But I forced myself to swallow the sandwich, washing it down with a cup of tea. I needed a lot of vitality to keep myself going until Abhinav recovered, and based on where he was currently, it seemed like it might take a while.

The room was dingy inside, with very little daylight seeping in; it felt cold, but oddly comforting. I latched the door and settled onto the bed, weary. My body was debilitated, but my mind was awake—aflush with adrenaline, constantly terrified and attentive, darting in countless directions, thinking of how suddenly life had come to this point and of all the possible turns it could take from here.

It was May 24, 2021. The day that I didn't know then would alter the course of everything that lay ahead of me.

Abhinav had been in the ICU for the past five days. And on a ventilator for the past forty-eight hours; so for two of those five days.

He was 33 years old; he had recently turned 33, in fact, just two months before. We had celebrated the milestone with his family to compensate for the year before, when a strict lockdown had compelled us to celebrate it between just the two of us with a slightly smudged cake. That was all we had been able to get our hands on amidst the chaos that engulfed the world then.

My mind was now incessantly replaying the events of the night before. Dr. Pawan, a family friend and a physician overseeing Abhinav's condition alongside the hospital doctors, had entrusted me with a task to record and text him Abhinav's vitals every two hours.

I had stationed myself outside the ICU, taking solace on the cold iron benches of the waiting hall, and every two hours, I'd rise silently and make my way to his bedside.

An intricate web of more than a dozen tubes, each intimately attached to a different part of Abhinav's body, converged onto a handful of monitors. I would run my eyes from one monitor to another, desperately trying to grasp and note every statistic that was being displayed.

Abhinav had been made to lie sideways to accommodate for the devices attached to him, to let them merge seamlessly with his body. The familiar contours of my husband seemed to be fading with this amalgamation. He was someone else, a kind of machine himself. I wanted to go near him, to touch him, to stroke his hair, to kiss his forehead, but I couldn't get myself to do it. My feet always froze at a distance from him. He had become a stranger whom I didn't recognize anymore. I couldn't place him in the depths of my memory; I couldn't find any similarities with the man in whose embrace I had slept countless nights.

I had texted the doctor, "Heart Rate 146, Oxygen 90, Blood Pressure 91/45, Passed 60 ml urine." (sic)

Every two hours, I entered the ICU with renewed optimism in my heart that the statistics I would find this time would be different, improved. My life was hanging by the numbers on the monitors alongside Abhinav's. Every small positive fluctuation rekindled hope within me, every negative fluctuation sank my heart deeper into despair. Through the night, his vitals had remained more or less stable.

As I lay in bed now, I made a mental checklist of tasks I needed to get done while I tried to drift off to sleep.

Apply for a long leave from the office, around two months; Abhinav will need a lot of time to recover

Talk to Abhinav's boss and apply for his leave as well

Transfer house help's salary online

Get some fresh clothes from the Gurgaon home

I was half asleep when someone knocked on the door. I woke up, startled. It was Abhinav's cousin, his chachi's daughter. "We need to get you to the hospital right away," she implored, her eyes brimming with tears.

My heart pounded in my chest and my body snapped to full attention. In desperation, I pleaded with sobbing shrieks, "What has happened, what has happened!? Why do I need to be there? This can't be true. Please tell me it is not true!"

In a futile attempt to shield me, she lied, "They just need you at the hospital for some paperwork." The tears in her eyes and the sadness in her mother's gaze, who had now joined us, betrayed her words.

But I chose to believe that lie, because if I could deny the reality long enough, if I could trick myself out of it, it could, by some sorcery, cease to be real. I remembered how I had signed several No Objection Certificates (NOCs), allowing the doctors to try different medications and procedures on Abhinav over the last several nights. Maybe they just need another NOC from me to try out a new treatment, I told myself.

The ten-minute drive to the hospital felt like an eternity. My body was frozen, pressed against the back seat by the window.

A tiny part inside of me, the part that was still rational, had already recognized the grim truth—that it wasn't paperwork that awaited me, that the inevitable had happened. I knew that Papa had already arrived at the hospital that morning, and he would have taken care of all necessary documents that required the attention of the family.

But I couldn't bear to confront that reality. I willed the drive to take as long as it could. Abhinav was alive until I made it to the hospital.

In all the fifteen days that we had been living this nightmare; from the moment Abhinav had been admitted to the hospital until the time he went on the ventilator, his death was never an acceptable, anticipated scenario. In all the horrific possibilities that had played out in my mind—him being in the hospital for months, not days; him being on life support; him having a mere 30% chance of survival—he had always returned home to us. Always, without fail.

Because Abhinav was a healthy young man and I believed his body possessed the ability to combat whatever the virus had unleashed upon it. Because I had seen much older men and women with pre-existing comorbidities recover from COVID-19.

But mainly because I believed in the rationality and balance of suffering, that everyone got a calculated and equitable amount of it. That my quota of tragedy had already been used up. That I had already lived through my worst, and this could only be a minor setback; Abhinav could never really die.

As soon as we reached the hospital, I sprinted towards the ICU. I found the ICU doors shut, the harried staff not letting anyone in. My eyes immediately located Papa, who was standing by the doors. His face was damp with tears, his eyes swollen. Through his sobs, he was saying something in broken sentences that I couldn't decipher in the middle of all the chaos.

But I couldn't deny it anymore. The love of my life had left me forever. All that I had ever wanted and all that I ever had, had been snatched away from me in the blink of an eye. I was all alone, once again; I had lost to fate, once again.

I felt the kind of acute, heart-wrenching agony I never knew existed. A crippling affliction took over my body; a merciless, unbearable pain, reaching the extremities of my being. The weight of a thousand mountains had suddenly collapsed on me, slowly crushing my bones into fine dust as I struggled to breathe. It was a piercing sorrow that I didn't recognize, not from the death of my father, not from the multiple other deaths that I had witnessed so far.

It was acute. It was unique to the point of being exquisite.

It is strange how you never get accustomed to the idea of death, how it never ceases to shock you, how it somehow unlocks a new level of devastation every time it touches your life.

I wanted to surrender to that piercing pain. I wanted to collapse and slide into a deep coma and never return from it. I wanted my spirit to leave my body and vanish somewhere deep into the cosmos. I thought of sprinting out of the hospital and jumping into the running traffic to end my life. I didn't want to stay alive and withstand what I knew was to come.

But none of that happened. Instead, my body lost all ability to do anything at all. I just stood there, outside the ICU doors, stunned and immobile, an ancient monolith unmoved for millennia.

In the midst of the hospital that was enveloped in relentless commotion, my world slowed down. A montage of the three years Abhinav and I had spent together—the laughter that echoed through our days, the excitement of reuniting after periods of long distance, our wedding day and the time we spent together during the COVID-19 lockdown, all flashed across my eyes. It was as if I was watching a trailer to a rom-com that had suddenly come to an unexpected and tragic end.

2

The Body vs the Life

I was desperate to be by Abhinav's side, but the nurses weren't allowing us in. The ICU was overwhelmed with capacity, and there were others whose condition had deteriorated that very morning. As I waited outside in the hospital hall, my gaze wandered to the other side of the translucent ICU doors. I noticed a group of doctors and nurses covered in blue plastic gear huddled around a bed, not an inch of their bodies visible. They were trying to revive a patient.

Unlike the haunted tranquillity of a typical hospital hallway, the hall here was filled with howling shrieks of grief coupled with the loud clamour of stretchers moving in and out of the ICU. Abhinav was not the only one who died that day in that hospital; our tragedy was not entirely unique.

I vividly remember witnessing scattered groups of unfamiliar faces, each huddled in a different corner of the hallway, their mournful cries drowning the room. I must have seen at least three stretchers carrying the deceased in tightly wound white cloth being strolled out of the ICU door. There was death everywhere I looked. If the world was supposed to end, it had to be then. If the human race was supposed to be wiped off the face of the earth, it had to be at that moment.

Soon enough, some of Abhinav's close relatives started showing up. There was some chatter about making arrangements and transporting the "body" to the cremation ground. It was appalling how suddenly Abhinav had stopped being a person and had become a "body" instead. I heard someone call out to Papa, "Make sure we remove all valuables from the body—rings, chains and other things."

I was disgusted. Who cared about the now-worthless valuables when Abhinav was going to be burned to ashes in a few hours? Why should anything else claim the superiority of remaining intact when he was not going to be? It should all be burned down with him. Our every valuable, every material possession, every single piece of my life should be rightly turned to ashes with him.

I controlled my exasperation to address their concern. "There is nothing on his body; he had removed his wedding band before coming to the hospital." It is the ring that I wear around my neck on a chain today.

I suppose that's why distant relatives need to show up at such occasions, to make more rational decisions and think about the practical next steps that demand attention, like removing pieces of jewellery from the body of the deceased person, booking a spot at the cremation ground, calling up other family members—things that seem insignificant to the rest of us who are just too numb and in disbelief of reality.

To top it all, the deaths during the second wave of COVID-19 faced additional hurdles to these practical next steps. Securing a spot in the cremation ground required phone calls, and ambulances were not readily available to transport the dead and their family.

After what felt like days but may have been an hour or two, Abhinav's nurse emerged from the ICU and requested us to be patient for a little longer as they needed time to "clean him up." While we waited in the hallway, drowned in agony, I noticed how others—some onlookers, some passersby, and some others whose loved ones were in the ICU and still alive, were all looking at us intently. They watched this tragic script unravel in front of their eyes, some with curiosity about what had happened and who had died, others with pity knowing what had happened and who had died. Still others looked at us with relief that it was us and not them who had come face-to-face with this tragedy.

I continued to sob, standing vulnerably in the hallway, my grief naked and exposed to their prying glares. I wanted them to look away. I wanted them to leave us to our misery.

An hour later, our nurse reappeared; we could go inside to see Abhinav, one person at a time.

Thinking back on all the deaths that I have witnessed thus far, I find myself in a peculiar quandary. I wonder whether or not one should see their loved ones after they pass away; before they are snatched away from you once and for all, before they cease to be treated as humans, before their bodies are wrapped and tied up in cloth like a parcel set for delivery to a faraway land.

One of Abhinav's close friends refused to see him. While the others pestered, he was adamant, "I don't want to see him in this state. I want to remember him as I have known him for most of his life, full of cheer and vitality."

I, on the other hand, couldn't stop myself from wanting to go inside. I knew I was putting a lot at stake; I was risking tarnishing the grinning image of him, etched in the depths of my mind, by whatever I was going to witness next. But then, how could I not say one last goodbye to my husband? How could I let go of this last opportunity to get a glimpse of his handsome face? How could I not want to touch him one last time?

Abhinav has been stationed at the very end of the long ICU room, which was lined with more than a dozen beds on both sides. As I walked past the other patients and numerous nurses, my eyes went straight to his bed, which was now concealed behind heavy brown curtains.

I parted the curtains and peeped inside. Still clothed in the hospital's purple gown, he rested on the right side of his body.

To my bare eyes, there seemed to be nothing wrong with him. He seemed perfectly fine, possibly in a deep slumber, but definitely not dead. Perhaps the nurses had "cleaned him up" so well that there were no visible signs of death on him.

The familiar beeping of the machines that I had grown so accustomed to hearing around him for the last couple of days had ceased. There were no tubes attached to him anymore. At that moment, he seemed more alive than he did while he was on the ventilator.

As soon as I was by his bed, I grabbed him by the side and started shaking him forcefully, all this while screaming, "Wake up, Abhinav. Wake up, I am here," hoping that my voice would reach him in some unknown depth and awaken him to consciousness. My 30-something brain, despite having gone through this multiple times, simply couldn't comprehend that he was not there. It couldn't understand, couldn't accept the dichotomy between "body" and "life." All it could process was—he is here, his whole body is here, how can he be dead? I found myself thinking, "Maybe, I just need to scream his name a bit louder or shake him a bit more violently to wake him up."

The concept of life leaving the body while the body perseveres for some time longer becomes difficult to fathom when you come face-to-face with it. The mind is perplexed because, to it, the body seems synonymous with life. If the body is here, without any major scars, then how could the life within not be?

While I continued to jerk Abhinav's body and scream in an effort to wake him up, the nurse came in and tried to pry me off him. Since Abhinav was COVID-19-positive, I wasn't supposed to be near him for long. But none of it mattered to me anymore; I wanted to hold him for as long as they would allow me to.

As I wrestled myself out of the nurse's grasp, I looked at her through the corner of my eyes. I noticed how her eyes had welled up with tears.

I stopped struggling with her momentarily as I became profoundly aware of what had transpired. I saw the horrors of my life reflected in her tear-filled eyes and slowly began to grasp the overwhelming extent of my misery.

It is strange how sometimes it is the impassioned reaction of a complete stranger to something that has happened to you that makes you realise the magnitude of a tragedy.

I wonder how many such deaths and deranged reactions of grieving relatives she had encountered over the last few months. I wonder if she felt particularly moved by our situation, since Abhinav was relatively young, or was she, in fact, a new nurse who had recently started witnessing deaths, and each death was equally devastating for her. I don't remember her face anymore, but her watered eyes come back to haunt me every once in a while. I wonder if she ever thinks about us and as often as I think about her.

As I jostled with her, I kissed Abhinav on his forehead one last time. I touched his still bouncy hair and whispered into his ear, "I will love you forever." And I meant those words with every ounce of my being. With the debilitating agony that throbbed my heart violently, I felt the kind of unquestioning love that was free from any need for reciprocation, that I might not have felt for him or anyone else before.

A year-and-a-half after his death, I don't know if I love him with the same ferocity as I loved him that day and in that moment as I walked away from him for the last time.

Part II

Days Before

3

The Wrath of COVID-19

It was early March 2020, and we had just returned from our short honeymoon in Goa.

Terrifying images of masked scientists and doctors in dimly-lit research laboratories and hospital rooms somewhere in a city called Wuhan in China began to surface across news channels and the internet. The channels played one particular clip on loop: that of a distressed Chinese doctor speaking to a camera in a muffled voice. The media claimed that he was warning the world about an outbreak of a potentially deadly virus that was rapidly spreading in China. There was other harrowing footage as well, of hospital rooms with doctors huddled around patients supposedly infected with the novel coronavirus, or SARS-CoV-2.

The visuals were chilling, but I, like most others, was largely unbothered; it all seemed too distant to be real, happening in some other part of the world, far removed from our lives. I dismissed it, convinced that this was another piece of sensational news coming out of China. Maybe even just a conspiracy theory, far from the truth.

But very quickly, in a matter of a couple of days, it all started becoming more and more real. The virus was spreading rapidly across the globe; it had already resulted in a wave of casualties in Italy and some other European countries.

Soon enough, news of the first cases being detected in India surfaced, and the next thing we knew, there were thousands of them. The virus had found its way into every nook and cranny, spreading like wildfire. Panic had started to grip the country.

The COVID-19 virus was unlike anything else seen before, rendering all existing vaccines and medicine ineffective against its onslaught. Scientists worldwide rallied in an effort to understand the virus, its symptoms and its lethality. Governments, faced with an adversary that knew no boundaries, grappled with the task of anticipating its impact and devising policies to control its spread.

What was known so far was that the virus was highly contagious. Once it infiltrated the human body, the infected person would initially show flu-like symptoms. Then, very quickly, the virus would invade the lungs, damaging them severely, leading to acute breathlessness and, ultimately, collapse if the required medical attention was not received in time.

Taking a cue from governments of other countries, India imposed a country-wide lockdown. The lockdown was a stark departure from anything that I had previously encountered. Having grown up in the strife-torn state of Jammu and Kashmir, I was no stranger to the disruptions caused by occasional *bandhs*. But this lockdown was nothing like the Jammu *bandhs*. Those meant that the traffic on the main roads was going to be restricted and the big markets would shut down, but life in the interiors of the city would carry on as usual. The current lockdown was several times stricter than the ones I knew.

A state of utter confusion, terror and fear had descended upon all of us. Supermarkets were thronged with people trying to stock up on provisions, and soon there was a scarcity of essential items. Many of my colleagues had started travelling back to their hometowns as offices began to shut down in the bigger cities. Who knew how long the lockdown would last for? A few weeks into it, the housing society that we were residing in imposed restrictions on stepping out of our flats and everything had to be delivered to our doorsteps, literally. We were placed under a sort of house arrest until further notice, shrinking our world to the confines of our four walls.

All of these developments—the surge in COVID-19 cases, the mounting global mortality toll, the frenzied scenes at the supermarkets, the abrupt shift to remote work—triggered my anxiety. Doom set upon me. I began to see it as the end of the world, the destruction of the human race. I would wake up jittery every morning, immediately reaching for my phone and frantically searching for "India COVID-19 Cases," "Jammu COVID-19 Cases," "Gurgaon COVID-19

Cases," "Delhi COVID-19 Cases." The numbers surged exponentially with each passing day, and so did my anxiety.

This anxiety manifested into vivid, haunting daydreams, in which it all culminated into something akin to an alien attack sequence from an apocalypse movie. I was consumed by a series of menacing images that flooded my brain all day—masses fleeing the city in a frenzy, buildings crumbling one after the other, abandoned children on the streets crying out for their lost parents—chaos all around. However, unlike the movies, it was not going to be man vs ape or man vs alien; it was going to be man vs man. The only way out, the only way to survive, was to decimate others. And unlike the movies, where there was always a hero who emerged against all odds to save the day, there was no hero who could save us from this particular apocalypse. Each one of us was on their own.

Abhinav, who was at the other end of the anxiety spectrum and always managed to take things in his stride, declared, "This is awesome; we are getting to spend so much time together. It is like an extended honeymoon!"

I was baffled, but also slightly impressed by his ability to adapt to this new way of living so seamlessly. How naturally it came to him, while I struggled tremendously.

He would wake up promptly at 7 am every day, follow an online workout routine and prepare a delightful breakfast for both of us, all this while being in an excellently cheerful mood. He would then dress up in business-casuals and start working at his desk that he had recently set up.

For me, on the other hand, each day was an uphill battle. I would somehow muster the strength to get out of bed, have a panic attack almost immediately and soon after, return to my bed and start working on my laptop begrudgingly, while still in my pyjamas.

When the weekend would finally arrive, Abhinav would slip into his cherished brown robe—his way of declaring that he had officially entered "weekend mode," and would remain in that robe all weekend long.

How could someone be so calm and unbothered amidst a global pandemic? His unwavering equanimity, which seemed so foreign, would astonish me on most days but also annoy me on some. I couldn't understand his zeal in such gloomy times. How could someone be so alien to sadness?

Perhaps that is why he was supposed to be in my life, to be the yin to my yang, to bring me back to the wonderful present that was unfolding around us as I drifted away to the tragic past or the uncertain future.

His presentness, his contentment with where we were and how we were, was indeed infectious. I found myself slowly catching it as I started relishing our routines while being locked up in our rented, two-bedroom apartment.

Together, by each other's side, we immersed ourselves in the rhythm of daily life. We were cooking together, cleaning together, exercising together. We were starting to live our lives together.

Abhinav was a man of routine. Every Friday evening, he would gather us both to plan our meals for the upcoming week. On Saturday afternoons, he would insist on ordering in to indulge in our weekly "cheat meals." While I would browse indecisively through menus of multiple restaurants to figure out what to order and where from, he would always order the same meal—a McDonald's Maharaja Mac, fries and a Coke.

Sunday movie nights had become a cherished ritual, and we took it seriously in the Agrawal household. We would transform our living room into a cosy haven, scented candles dotting the scene. To set the mood just right, I would prepare my signature vegetable Maggi and we would couple that with an ordered-in dessert.

Our choice in movie genres couldn't have been more dissimilar, sparking frequent disagreements. He introduced me to the Mission Impossible series, the Matrix series, and the ghastly TV show *The Boys*. And, I made him suffer through a series of rom-coms.

However, my favourite part of our movie nights was never the movies themselves. As the movie played, I would lie down with my head resting on Abhinav's lap, and soon his fingers would start weaving through my hair while he enthusiastically jabbered on about the easter eggs in the movie, a concept that was completely foreign to me before I met him.

And just like that, I didn't care about the movie's plot anymore. I didn't care about the rising numbers of COVID-19 infections anymore. I was at peace, then and there; the world outside our little cocoon slowly faded away.

We had our first fight over responsibilities of household chores, and we made up. We started imagining our lives together in the near future—where we would travel to once the COVID-19 restrictions are lifted, how we would furnish our house, which gym we wanted to join and the gift I wanted from him on my next birthday.

We started dreaming about our lives beyond the near future as well—how many children we wanted to have and when, what age we wanted to retire at, where we would settle down eventually.

As time elapsed, my worries about the pandemic began to wane. Although I still kept a track of the numbers, it did not agitate me as much. It seemed that the initial fears about the pandemic were exaggerated and the virus wasn't as deadly as it was originally perceived to be. In India, the mortality rates remained low, and the government soon declared that we had been successful in combating the pandemic.

With this positive turn of events, a newfound cheer spread across the country. Offices and markets gradually reopened, and the streets started bustling with life once again. As a sense of normalcy returned, Abhinav and I eagerly started picking up where we had left off, resuming shopping for our home which had been temporarily halted by the pandemic and the ensuing lockdown.

4

The Last One Remaining

It was August 2020 when COVID-19 cases began to spike in India. People were reported getting infected to the extent that they needed hospitalisation due to rapidly falling oxygen saturation levels. News of hospital bed shortages and patients' relatives scrambling for oxygen cylinders to save their loved ones was all over. Lakhs of new cases were detected every day and daily mortalities began reaching triple digits.

Back home in Jammu, my buji—my father's only sister and his only surviving sibling, the only one among the four of them who had lived to see sixty—got infected with the virus. We all panicked. She had several comorbidities: thyroid, diabetes, high blood pressure; the virus could potentially be life-threatening for her.

My cousins in Jammu were being pushed from pillar to post trying to get her proper treatment, and I was consumed by a deep sense of helplessness miles away in Delhi. The situation in smaller towns was worse, owing to a much weaker medical infrastructure. There was an acute scarcity of hospital beds. Even if beds were available, the hospitals didn't have an adequate supply of oxygen with them. In the absence of amenities, patients were being isolated in wards and left to fend for themselves. My family was left with no choice but to treat her on their own with the help of online consultation with doctors.

I would get daily updates on her condition, which seemed to be deteriorating with every passing day. After struggling for two weeks—scrambling for oxygen cylinders, administering nebulizers at home and arranging for scarce medicines—she succumbed to the virus.

An era had ended with her.

I wouldn't say that I was particularly close to Buji; we seldom talked. But I was in complete awe of her. Through the years of chaos, tragedy and conflict among my father's large, extended family, she had been the pillar of strength and solidarity that had held us all together. She had assumed the position of the matriarch after the death of all three of her brothers, my dad and my two chachas. All our major family decisions went through her. Decisions regarding marriage, naming newborns, buying and selling family property or jewellery—all of it had to have her final stamp of approval.

In the absence of our fathers, and in light of our docile mothers, she had unwillingly, yet unequivocally, risen to be the head of our extended family.

My allegiance towards her grew at the time that she took charge of my wedding. She couldn't do a lot physically but she ensured there were no gaps in the wedding preparations. In fact, it was her and Fufaji, her husband, who did my *kanyadaan* (a symbolic tradition performed by the bride's family, blessing and 'giving her hand' to the groom and his family) to Abhinav and the Agrawal family.

With all her growing health issues, her gait had slowed down considerably, but her zeal remained unmatchable. There was something powerful about her aura that commanded respect, not just from people in our family but also from everyone else who knew her.

It was heartbreaking that I couldn't go to Jammu to say one last goodbye to her. It was heartbreaking that the last surviving member of my father's family was now gone. A generation had ended, their legacy, now our responsibility. I can't speak for my cousins, but I didn't feel ready for it.

However, what was most heartbreaking was the fact that someone whose life was a constant celebration, who made sure that her guests were always well attended, well fed and gifted, that person was bid farewell without much fanfare. She took her last breath at her home and was carried away in an ambulance accompanied just by her husband and son.

I said my goodbye to her through a video call, as my chacha's daughter climbed up the terrace of Buji's house. She was wrapped head-to-toe in plastic and was being taken away on a stretcher.

I grieved in Gurgaon, away from my family, but thankfully I had Abhinav by my side to support me through it.

***

A few months later, the situation started stabilising again. Abhinav and I got a chance to visit my family in Jammu in December 2020, almost a year after we were married. Abhinav, as usual, charmed his way into everyone's hearts and I gave myself a little pat on the back for landing such a funny, humble and kind husband. I showed him around my city, the places close to my heart, my school, my college, my hangout spots. I was on a dopamine high.

There was also promising news of vaccines being developed by major pharmaceutical companies globally. They were soon made available for senior citizens in March 2021 and were slated to be opened up to younger adults in a couple of months. Daily infections had started decreasing, and markets and other public places began opening up again.

But soon enough, in April 2021, a second wave caused by the COVID-19 variant, Delta, suddenly hit India. We figured we should lock ourselves down, just like the last time, and wait until the situation simmered down. But this time around, we decided to go into lockdown with Papa and Mom, Abhinav's parents, in their Delhi house.

Papa and Mom lived in Delhi, about thirty kilometres away from where Abhinav and I had rented a place in Gurgaon, to be closer to our jobs. It worked perfectly for us—we were close to our work but also not too far from them. Amidst the lockdowns and the border shutdowns between Delhi and Gurgaon, we tried to be with Abhinav's parents as much as we could. With the second wave, we reasoned that there was no point in living separately in Gurgaon, if we were going to be working from home anyway.

It also started becoming evident very quickly that things were going to be much worse this time around. This variant was much more virulent than the previous variants and was, thus, spreading more rapidly. The people too, had become relatively negligent. Based on what we had experienced during the first wave, the prevailing wisdom was that the virus could only be life-threatening if you had comorbidities or if you were past a certain age. For the young and the healthy, its severity was perceived to be similar to that of the common cold.

And yet, the daily numbers kept escalating. They were exponentially higher than those in the first wave. There were many more casualties each day and a bigger pandemonium.

Our TV screens were again bombarded with terrifying visuals non-stop —people jostling in endless lines to secure oxygen cylinders for their families, relatives scrambling outside hospitals for beds. There were morbid images of cemeteries full of hundreds of pyres that were burning simultaneously, blinding smoke billowing off them forming despairing clusters of dark clouds.

Then there was this one horrifying image circulating across newspapers, TV channels and all over social media—an image that became the face of COVID-19 in India. It was a picture of a saree-clad middle-aged woman trying to resuscitate her husband by breathing into his mouth in the back of an auto-rickshaw. It was heartbreaking to see. I couldn't shake off the scene from my head for several days.

Social media was abuzz with information about and requests for plasma, bed availability in hospitals and contact numbers of suppliers of oxygen cylinders and concentrators. Thousands of migrant workers were shown on TV screens walking back home to their villages, for days at a stretch, as all public transport had come to a halt. Without work, it had become difficult for them to sustain themselves in the cities.

There was death and misery all around.

We watched all of it unravel from a distance, from the comfort of our home. There was a part of me that had soothed me into thinking that this couldn't possibly happen to us. Like all the other terrible news that plays on TV, I reassured myself that this is something happening to other families, to other people. I had become delusional; I was so blinded by the current bliss of my life that my cruel past had become obscure now. It didn't unnerve me, it didn't caution me anymore.

I had long forgotten the fact that the worst does happen, and sometimes, it happens to you again.

A couple of days later, Papa and Mom started showing COVID-19-like symptoms.

5

COVID-19 Got Us

It all started with a sore throat and a runny nose. We tried to reassure ourselves: maybe it is not the virus, maybe it is just a cold that Papa and Mom had caught due to the changing weather.

However, they wanted to be cautious, so they isolated themselves in their room.

We started closely monitoring their fever and other symptoms. We would place food, water, medicines and other essentials that they needed at their door, and pick the empty dishes up after they were finished.

A day or two later, they alerted us that they were both running high fevers. We again reassured ourselves that those were just symptoms of a common cold. How could they have been infected? All four of us had been locked indoors for a fortnight now; they couldn't possibly have contracted the virus from inside the house.

We thought of waiting it out some more to see how the situation would progress.

When their fever persisted for two more days, we had to get them tested for COVID-19. To our horrors, the tests came back positive. Over a phone consultation, the doctor prescribed them some mild medication, mostly consisting of paracetamol for the fever and ibuprofen for body aches.

We waited, our fingers crossed, hoping they would start getting better soon. Amidst all the anxiety, there was some solace in the fact that Papa had received both the doses of the COVID-19 vaccine and Mom had received one.

But it all started going south thereafter. Their fever showed no signs of relenting, and the virus continued to enfeeble them. Despite some stability in their oxygen saturation initially, it had started to sink concerningly below 90%.

Abhinav and I panicked; we needed to take action soon before the situation worsened. We realised that our home treatment plan was proving to be inadequate. We required an in-person doctor consultation to evaluate their condition and get guidance accordingly.

While Abhinav drove them both to the hospital, I began gathering information about oxygen cylinders, hospital beds and medicines. By this point, we had become acutely aware of the shortage of these essentials and I wanted us to be prepared in case Mom's or Papa's situation deteriorated.

Over the next few days, Abhinav drove them back and forth to the hospital a couple more times. He would contact me every few hours to give updates; things were looking terribly grim. I kept reminding him to take precautions for his own safety as well: "Wear your double masks and PPE kit at all times," "Sanitise everything you touch," "Don't touch your mask with your hands." I was aware that it was challenging for him to prioritise his own well-being given that he was running around in the scorching heat of Delhi, wearing a stifling PPE suit, under immense stress. But I kept nagging him, to the point of him getting annoyed.

This continued for a couple of days, until one morning, at around 6 am, Mom's situation suddenly started deteriorating. She woke up completely out of breath. Her oxygen had plummeted to 80% saturation and was crashing rapidly. We had arranged for an oxygen concentrator at home, but it was proving to be insufficient. She needed to be admitted to a hospital immediately.

Panic seized all of us. Papa frantically started reaching out to friends and family to help find a bed in a hospital. Meanwhile, Mom continued to struggle, each breath becoming more laborious than the last, as she desperately clung to the support of the concentrator.

Luckily, before anything untoward could happen, Papa was able to secure a bed for Mom at a hospital. Without wasting any time, he and Abhinav immediately rushed to admit her.

That day, when Abhinav returned home, his state of mind reflected starkly on his face. I had never seen him so tense before. I wanted to talk to him, to tell him that I was there for him, that he was not alone, but he kept avoiding me. At night, he insisted that he should sleep in the living room given that he had been out all day and might have been exposed to the virus. But I refused; I had a valid reason. He had been in a PPE kit throughout the day, there was very little chance that he had caught something. He agreed, but still insisted on sleeping facing the opposite end of the bed, my feet facing his face and his facing mine, ensuring that we were still maintaining some safe distance.

An unfamiliar, eerie silence enveloped us as we lay wide awake on opposite ends of our bed. The weight of his troubled thoughts was unbearable, leaving me restless and unable to sleep. I wanted him to open up his agony to me, but I couldn't pester him. I was reminded of how poorly it had turned out the last time around.

We were dating at the time when his grandmother had passed away. I had sensed how heartbroken he was and had tried to comfort him, to speak to him, but he would not engage with me. In response to his grief, he withdrew, growing increasingly irritated by my persistent questioning.

Men and their intrinsic need to repress their feelings.

This time though, as moments of unsettling silence passed, he finally spoke, without any nudge from me. He was barely audible, as if he was afraid to voice his fears, "I was very scared today. What if something had happened to Mom? What if we weren't able to arrange for a hospital bed in time? We could have lost her."

I got up from my side of the bed and inched closer to him. We were now facing each other. I reassured him, "She will be fine, everyone will be fine soon, nothing is going to happen. We will get through this together." I was saying that to him as much as I was saying it to myself.

He looked at me and made a request, "Do you mind stroking my back?" I nodded, recognizing that he wanted to be comforted. I began to caress his back gently, just as I would comfort an infant. Long, tender strokes all the way from his forehead, through the waves of his thick hair, down to his back, and then back to his forehead again. As I continued to do so, he began to open up about the immense weight he felt, the weariness that consumed him, the overwhelming fear of losing his parents.

I said nothing in response. I wanted his thoughts to flow unbridled. But I understood that stinging feeling of fear very well; I had had a brush with it not so long before. How could I ever forget that feeling in a million years? The soul-crushing fear of losing a parent and having to live with the guilt of not having done enough to save them—I hadn't known a feeling worse than that.

The following day, while Abhinav was visiting Mom in the hospital, my body started aching severely, and I knew without a doubt that the virus had taken hold of me as well.

Based on the information available off the internet and my conversation with a family doctor, I figured I had to wait for six more days to understand how the infection was progressing. I game-planned with Abhinav on how we would proceed in case things started deteriorating for me as well.

Now Abhinav was the only one in the family who hadn't been exposed to the virus yet, or at least that's what we assumed then. We decided to isolate him in an empty flat upstairs that belonged to the neighbours.

Soon, it became clear that my infection was not that severe; my oxygen saturation levels were not fluctuating as much. The only symptoms I had were fever and body aches, which, too, were receding with each passing day. By this time, Papa had almost recovered and Mom was recovering fast in the hospital.

The developments brought relief to Abhinav, and I could sense the familiar jollity in his voice returning as we spoke over the phone. As my body aches and fever started receding, I grew increasingly impatient to be by his side. This was, by far, the longest we had been apart since our wedding.

For the next few days, every morning, Abhinav would visit the hospital to check on Mom. Then, upon returning, he would promptly come downstairs to see Papa and me. He would stand outside the meshed door of the flat, keeping a careful distance. His face would be concealed behind a mask. I would stand on the other side of the door, also masked.

We were like new lovers again, brimming with excitement to get a blurred glimpse of one another; yearning to be in each other's embrace, but separated by a flimsy door erected by a ruthless pandemic that stood resolute between us.

At the time, I didn't have the faintest idea of what was to come; I couldn't foresee that there was no going back to normal from here. I didn't know that, despite our separation, I should cherish this time wholeheartedly. For it was somewhere in these moments that my joy was about to peak.

A few days before Mom was about to be discharged from the hospital, Abhinav came downstairs to see us and announced, "I am running a fever."

6

In the Hospital

Iwas not alarmed when Abhinav declared that he was showing symptoms of the infection. It was inevitable; he was the one who had been the most exposed while running around a city potent with disease.

There was already some news making rounds about how the new Delta strain was life-threatening not just to aged people with underlying comorbidities but also to the young and healthy. Fear briefly set in, but I rationalised that if Abhinav had indeed contracted the virus, it would likely be the same strain that we had all been exposed to. His symptoms should be mild as well, and he should recover from it in not more than a week.

In a couple of hours, I received a text from him from the apartment above, stating, "I am doing my exercise routine. Maybe breaking a sweat will help me shake off this fever."

It didn't.

We moved him downstairs with us, recognizing that there was no point in keeping him isolated in a separate apartment anymore since we were all infected now. And as I was recovering fast, I figured I could take better care of him.

By then, I was well versed with the COVID-19 drill—the drill that almost every Indian household was familiar with at that time: the medicines to take, the breathing exercises to perform, the steam inhalation to clear out the nasal blockage, the monitoring of the patient's fever, oxygen saturation and pulse every 3-4 hours. And, finally, waiting it out for the standard five-six days, closely tracking how the different parameters fluctuated.

Abhinav's fever ran exceedingly high for the first few days, surpassing the levels of what I had experienced throughout my own illness. We attempted to manage it through higher doses of paracetamol. The fever would subside for an hour or two with the medication but would soon, and rapidly, escalate to 103 degrees. This pattern was alarming given my fever had been quite tameable with the medication.

It became evident that his infection and mine were not following the same trajectory and were not of the same severity. Still, we decided to adhere to our six-day wait period.

When his fever did not recede even after five days and he was drowsy with it almost all the time, we decided to get a CT scan of his lungs. It was recommended by our doctor to evaluate the severity of his infection.

The results indicated moderate to severe infection, similar to Mom and Papa. The doctor examined the test's outcome and suggested that as long as Abhinav's oxygen saturation levels remained within a normal range, we could continue to monitor him within the confines of our home.

To our dismay, the very next day, his oxygen levels began to drop below 90%. I rushed to Papa and alerted him.

Looking back at everything that unfolded thereafter, I often think about what would have happened had I not panicked that day. What if we had not taken Abhinav to the hospital and instead taken a different course of action? Would he still have been alive?

The doctors were anyway navigating uncharted territories and nobody knew a hundred percent what needed to be done. Much of the treatment was experimental at that time. The efficacy of drugs and treatments was being celebrated one day and then dropped the next.

What if I had heeded Abhinav's stance, who was absolutely reluctant to go to the hospital? What if we had explored the option of managing his condition at home with some external consultation? How oblivious I was of the fact that I was standing at a crossroads in my life that could lead to two completely divergent paths. The decision I was taking would thrust me down a road marked by ceaseless anguish and an even greater burden of remorse.

Abhinav was groggy but remained adamant that hospitalisation was not required. I found myself in tears, pleading to him to not resist. Incidentally, on the same day, Mom was supposed to get discharged from the same hospital we were planning on taking Abhinav to. Papa drove Abhinav to the hospital and brought Mom back home. It was as if we were trading with the devil, one life for another.

I chose not to accompany them, convinced that Abhinav was now in capable hands and would receive the same kind of treatment as Mom. I held to the belief that following Mom's recovery timeline, he should also be back at home soon.

A lot had already transpired in a matter of days, and now Abhinav was in hospital as well. It had just been two weeks since our ordeal began, and yet I felt extremely weary—partly because of the quick turn of events, and partly due to the toll that the infection had taken on my own body. My heart yearned for the familiar routines of our life back in Gurgaon and wanted to return to the comfort of that mundanity.

I recall dialling Abhinav's number shortly after Papa returned from the hospital. A torrent of anxious queries poured out of me: "How are you feeling?" "Have they started you on medicines?" "Are you comfortable in the room?"

He placed my call on hold, leaving me momentarily confused. But immediately after, my phone buzzed with a message. He had sent me a picture of him. In the selfie that he had probably just taken, he was wearing a purple and white chequered hospital robe and giving me a thumbs up. While it didn't completely pacify me, it did manage to bring a brief smile on my face.

Months later, when I stumbled upon that picture among the multitude of X-rays and medical reports in my phone's gallery, I meticulously archived it in a private folder. It's not that I don't have enough pictures of him—my phone is brimming with countless photos of him scattered all across my gallery. Yet, it is this particular picture that is more precious to me than any other picture of him; it is the last tangible memory I have of his smiling face.

I texted him back, "Just follow the doctor's advice, don't resist them too much. They know the best. Get better soon and come back quickly," along with several hearts and kisses emoticons.

I recalled getting into a petty fight with him a couple of weeks back, on how I needed space from him, given we were always together. I desperately wanted to take my words back. I was absolutely wrong; I couldn't bear being apart from him even for a single moment now. I didn't want any space anymore. I wanted him to be with me right there and then.

I received a text back from him, "Don't you worry. This will all be over soon. Once I am back, we will both return to our Gurgaon home," almost as if he had read my mind.

The next day, Papa and I visited Abhinav at the hospital. His condition seemed to have improved. He was no longer drowsy with fever but was definitely still annoyed with us for admitting him to the hospital. Wearing his low intensity oxygen mask that was pumping around four-five litres of oxygen in his body, he was fully engrossed in his phone. I was relieved to see him looking a bit better already.

Satisfied, we proceeded to the doctor's cabin to discuss Mom's medicines. In our mind, Abhinav was looking and, thus, feeling better. We had concluded that he was out of danger and on his path to recovery. However, the doctor's remarks caught us off-guard. "I will review her medicines later. Right now, we need to focus on Abhinav. His oxygen is dropping rapidly despite the steroids we gave him. We need to immediately start him on some additional treatments."

My heart began to race as panic set in.

On the recommendation of the doctor, we began arranging for the plasma of a recovered COVID-19 patient for infusion. Papa began reaching out to several sources, and many of Abhinav's friends who had recently recovered from COVID-19 also volunteered to help. Fortunately, soon enough we were able to locate a plasma source in a distant blood bank in the centre of Gurgaon. Without losing a minute, we rushed and brought it to the hospital.

However, the very next day, plasma therapy was taken off the list of approved COVID-19 treatments by the panel of doctors leading the national guidance on the pandemic. Nonetheless, we remained hopeful, especially Papa, that it could still prove beneficial. He reassured us, "My friend's son, who is of Abhinav's age, was also infected with severe COVID-19, but he started getting better after the plasma infusion therapy. You will see, Abhinav's condition will also start to improve soon. We just need to give it two-three days."

However, our hearts sank when, even after three days, there were no signs of improvement.

After the plasma treatment, the doctors began recommending medicines which were among the buzzwords of COVID-19 treatment at that time—favipiravir, remdesivir and what not. As soon as the doctor would prescribe them, Papa and I would rush to obtain them. Many of those medicines had scarce availability and were being sold at ten-to-hundred times their original price in the black market.

But none of it seemed to help. Abhinav's oxygen saturation kept spiralling downwards despite all the medication. He was now required to wear a much stronger mask, pumping around fifteen litres of oxygen at once to aid his breathing.

7

Not Getting Any Better

At home, I was growing exceedingly restless without Abhinav, so I decided to sneak into the hospital. The hospital staff, at first, was reluctant to allow me in for more than a couple of hours due to safety concerns, but because I pleaded that I had just recovered from COVID-19 and must have developed antibodies, they permitted me to stay for extended hours. Also, the hospital was in such chaos at the time that it was relatively easy to flout the social distancing regulations.

I settled on to the visitors' bench beside Abhinav's bed. Being by his side gave me a lot of respite and I felt more in control of the situation.

The initial four-five days were relatively smooth. Abhinav continued breathing through his oxygen mask and would spend his days watching *Rick and Morty* on his phone while lying on his stomach. The doctors had advised that position to help maintain his oxygen levels. Periodically, I would make him take breaks from his binge-watching and help him with his breathing exercises.

Occasionally, he would remove his mask and ask me to check his oxygen levels without its support. The oxygen levels would crash to sub-70% saturation and he would start gasping almost immediately. This would dishearten us both, but we would never utter a word of distress to each other. Things were going to be fine after all. They *had* to be fine.

During the time that we spent together in the hospital ward, Abhinav and I continued our usual conversations about our future, which, at that point in time, was still intact. We would talk about taxes to be filed, bathroom fixtures that required repair, the car servicing that was soon due. Sometimes, we would also gossip about his roommates in the ward.

Abhinav's room had a bed adjacent to his, separated by curtains from his side of the room. Initially, it was occupied by a young man in his early twenties, who would mostly sleep and keep to himself, and later by a middle-aged man who would keep pressing the nurse-call buzzer all day long to complain about the food, the staff's negligence and the medicines. In hushed tones and soft chuckles, we would joke about his tantrums.

When I look back at our three years of relationship and over a year of marriage, I find that it was during this time, in the hospital, that I felt closest to Abhinav. Until now, we were just a carefree young couple living together under a roof, unravelling one another and our idiosyncrasies slowly; with no care in the world and no real responsibilities towards each other or anyone else. But being together in the hospital at this difficult time had suddenly accelerated our relationship by decades. In an unexpected way, these moments of turmoil had brought us together like none of the joyous moments of the past had.

Amidst all of this, death, at no point in time, was on our minds.

In hindsight, I often wonder if we should have had a conversation about 'What if the inevitable were to happen?' There are moments today when I am filled with an overwhelming sense of remorse at not using our time together to articulate to Abhinav what he truly meant to me—how he was the sun around which my world revolved, how the joy that he had brought to me was incomparable, how my life would lose all its meaning without him by my side.

Sometimes, quite selfishly, I find myself wishing that in those moments he should have shared his unfulfilled dreams with me. The ones that, maybe, he would want me to pursue, in case something inadvertent were to happen. Something that would have helped me anchor my life without him, that would have given me a sense of direction at a time when I felt completely lost.

Sometimes, I indulge in the frivolous thought that he should have left behind a trail of notes—just like Gerry did in the movie *P.S. I Love You* to guide his wife, Holly, through her journey of grief and rediscovering herself, after his death. Like a deranged woman, I had desperately tried to look for messages from him after he passed away. I would often dream of finding those notes tucked away in some corner of our home, or saved in a folder on his phone somewhere. Each one, I dreamt to be a testament of his love for me and a guided path towards healing.

I recognize that this is a thing of fiction; and that wishing that Abhinav should have been thinking about giving direction to my life, while his own was hanging by a thread is selfish of me, at best. In reality, any such tragedy was beyond the realms of our imaginations. Our mind clung to only one narrative—Abhinav is young and healthy and nothing could possibly happen to him.

But with each passing day, he was growing increasingly feeble. We were all alarmed at the rate at which his body was deteriorating. His lips persistently looked severely parched. The multiple blood draws from various spots on his arms had begun to leave deep blue wounds; I made a mental note to bring some Betadine from home to apply on them. Dandruff flakes had started showing up for the very first time on his scalp. Again, I noted to myself that he needs a good head wash once he is back home.

At night, when he would be sound asleep, I would lay wide awake on the bench beside him, never taking my eyes off him, desperately hoping for the recovery to start the next morning. "Tomorrow is the day when the cycle of deterioration will begin to reverse. Tomorrow is the day when the virus will start subsiding." A constant chant played inside of me.

Continuing into the night, I would attempt to assess his symptoms and condition on my phone, trying to consume every little piece of information on the topic online, clicking through to find hope in the endless array of research articles available.

Reading the small font under the harsh light of my phone, I would frantically Google for "COVID-19 pneumonia and its severity," "Efficacy of remdesivir," "Side effects of steroids," "How to know if the COVID-19 infection is life threatening?" Eventually, exhaustion would overcome me, and I'd drift off to sleep.

The hospital, however, never slept. Through the night, nurses would make their rounds every few hours. They would show up to monitor Abhinav's oxygen levels and refill water in the machine that was supplying him the oxygen. Their movements and sounds would wake me up. Almost instinctively, I would reach out for my mini-oximeter and place it on Abhinav's index finger to measure his readings, only to be disappointed. Attempting to settle back onto the bench and hoping to reclaim my sleep, my mind would be plagued with dread. This couldn't be happening!

Each new morning arrived with an anxious wait for Abhinav's doctor, who would typically show up at around 9 am. He would go through Abhinav's reports and inquire, "How are you feeling?" to which Abhinav would always respond pensively, "I am feeling good." He would never complain about breathlessness or any other discomfort that he was experiencing, or direct any frustration at the doctor. I, on the other hand, would be consumed by a strong urge to vent my resentment, wanting to lash out, "Nothing you are doing is working! He is not getting any better! Help us!!!"

The doctor would then review Abhinav's reports a little more, pause and advise, "Continue with your breathing exercises." This would agonise me further. How were those breathing exercises expected to help Abhinav fight a lethal virus that had caused mayhem worldwide!

Finally, the doctor would proceed to instruct the nurses to make some alterations to Abhinav's medication. As he would walk out of the ward, I would trail behind him, desperately seeking clarity on what was *really* happening and bombarding him with questions which I couldn't get myself to ask in front of Abhinav. Unfortunately, the doctor would yield only a limited amount of information.

Returning to the ward with my nerves on edge, I would attempt to dissect Abhinav's reports myself. I would meticulously scrutinise the readings, most of which were beyond my comprehension. But because the reports typically also include defined normal ranges for each of the parameters, I could decipher that almost each and every reading was falling significantly outside those norms.

I would also try to comprehend the X-ray of his lungs, comparing it with the previous day's images, hopelessly trying to find a glimmer of hope in the clouded film of plastic that was handed to me daily. I attempted over and over again to deceive myself into believing that his situation was improving, "Today's X-ray shows less cloudiness on the right lung as compared to yesterday's; maybe this new drug is working." I would then take pictures of his reports and share them with everyone who, I believed, could potentially offer some valuable guidance on the ongoing treatment, and also with Papa and Mom, who would, in turn, share them with their own contacts.

Relatives and friends buzzed my phone constantly, anxious for updates. "Is he being given enough steroids?" "Is he being given too many steroids?" "Is he being given xyz medication?" "He shouldn't be given the xyz medicine," "Is he wearing the mask correctly?" "Share his reports with us, and we can consult another specialist."

Each person had their own version of what the best course of action was, and I would find myself overwhelmed by the avalanche of suggestions and opinions that were coming my way. While I held immense faith in the expertise of the hospital's doctors, hearing the multitude of perspectives from friends and family made me panic and question—Was Abhinav receiving the right treatment? Was this hospital and medical team the right fit for him? And also, was I really capable of making these decisions for him?

I felt utterly exhausted. Every moment felt like an unrelenting battle, one I feared I was losing with each passing day. I couldn't rest, I couldn't take my eyes off Abhinav even for a moment. Any oversight, any lapse, any misguided action, even the slightest delay could potentially put his life in jeopardy.

Abhinav continued to watch his shows on his phone with his oxygen mask tightly secured. He looked fine on the face of it, but under all of it, his condition was getting worse by the day. He was unable to talk at a stretch and would be out of breath by the end of his sentences. Simple movements like lying down from sitting or sitting upright from lying down were now arduous tasks. It would take him several minutes and someone's support to stabilise after changing positions. Standing upright on his feet was entirely out of the question; he had to rely on a wheelchair to move between rooms for tests that needed to be conducted.

I couldn't believe the nightmare we were living. I was losing my healthy husband by the day to the virus and nothing we were doing was proving to be of any help. I desperately waited for the moment when all the medicines and treatment would start working, I desperately waited for a miracle to happen.

It was in the middle of the night on May 18, 2021, that Abhinav's condition worsened. His oxygen levels plummeted to sub-80%, despite the strong oxygen mask. From what I had gathered so far, such a drastic fall in oxygen saturation levels posed the risk of an imminent collapse. I ran to the on-call doctor and begged him to admit Abhinav to the ICU.

8

Not a Saint After All

The ICU at our hospital, much like a lot of the ICUs across the country during that period, was overwhelmed and operating above capacity. There were no beds available at immediate notice. The on-call doctor recommended a temporary solution—we move Abhinav to the emergency room where he could get access to a BiPAP machine while we waited to secure a bed for him in the ICU.

Abhinav's lungs had deteriorated to the extent that they could only be sustained through a BiPAP machine. The device was capable of pumping high volumes of oxygen into the body, much higher than the oxygen mask that Abhinav was currently using.

I accompanied him as he was strolled in a wheelchair from his ward on the second floor to the emergency room on the ground floor.

The BiPAP machine was frightening to look at. Its two sturdy rubber belts were strapped across Abhinav's face to keep the mask fitted and stable, while a broad tube protruding from its middle pumped oxygen into his mouth at an extremely high pressure.

Abhinav was unable to endure the machine; the pressure was unbearable. The moment the doctors would affix the mask to his face, he would erupt into desperate cries directed at the medical team, "I am drowning in it, take it off!" The doctors attempted strapping the mask back on again every few minutes, but without much success. It was distressing to see Abhinav in so much pain. But I didn't know what else to do; this was the only way we could save his lungs from collapsing.

The emergency room was on the same floor as the ICU. Once Abhinav was somewhat settled in, I began pacing back and forth between the two units. In one, I would ensure that he was stable, and in the other, I would inquire with the nurses about the availability of a bed.

At the time, an ICU bed getting vacant typically implied one of two scenarios: either someone was being discharged after their lungs had reasonably recovered, or someone had died. Given the immense complications emanating from the Delta variant and the prolonged nature of recovery from it, in most cases—if not all—ICU beds only became available in the second scenario.

I was now out of the sheltered privacy and the relative tranquillity of the ward and in the midst of the chaos and commotion of the waiting hall. Positioned between the ICU and the emergency room, and adjacent to the large open entrance of the hospital, the waiting hall was lined with several rows of iron benches and was consumed with the unrelenting anxious energy of the relatives of the sick.

I was likely in extreme shock. Yet, I had to find ways to ground myself to think logically about what needed to be done next. Abhinav's worsening situation despite the rigorous treatment continued to dishearten me.

Soon, it was dark, and the unsettling nocturnal sky that I had managed to shield myself from, while behind the closed doors of the ward, now lay exposed before me in all its glory. There was a thunderstorm on most nights that I spent in the waiting hall. It roared like carnage was soon to descend upon earth; it would come and go across several nights, and my anxieties rode along with it.

Each time the storm calmed, a spark of hope glimmered in me about Abhinav's recovery. But the next day, when the skies would rumble again with torrential rain and furious lightning, my heart would sink for the fear of all the devastation that was to come.

That particular night, when Abhinav was moved to the emergency ward, I seated myself in the waiting hall, rapt with attention to everything that transpired across both the ICU and the emergency room. At around 2 am, the loud, anguished cries of a woman coming from outside the ICU pierced the stillness. Alarmed, I rushed to find out what was happening.

A 50-something year old woman stood wailing outside the ICU doors, pounding her chest violently with her fists, lamenting, "He left me! What will I do now! My life is over! Oh God, what has happened!" Beside her, stood two young men. Their tears flowed freely as they attempted to console her. The woman then collapsed to her knees as her chest-thumping grew even more intense while the two men tried to lift her up, but all in vain.

I could tell from her sobs that her husband, who had been in a critical state for several days and was admitted in the ICU, had passed away. My heart briefly swelled with sorrow for her misfortune. But then, almost immediately, my thoughts shifted focus and my mind began to tick—A bed in the ICU must have become available, I should rush to grab it before anyone else does.

I dashed to the ICU in-charge's cubicle and positioned myself behind the glass panel that separated us. I requested, almost discreetly, "It seems like someone has died in the ICU. Has a bed become available? My husband has been put up in the emergency room while we wait for an ICU bed. Could we get him moved there fast, now?"

The man looked up momentarily from his paperwork and met my gaze with what can only be described as a mix of indifference and disgust. He responded as he went back to his work, "Ma'am, a person has just died. We have to attend to some formalities before we can move your husband. Allow us some time."

Maybe I struck him as inconsiderate, unkind, even inhumane. It didn't matter. All that mattered in that moment was grabbing the now-vacant bed before anyone else could snatch it away. Nobody knew when the next bed would become available.

Until this precise moment in my life, I had upheld kindness and empathy towards others as my most cherished virtues. I took immense pride in the fact that compassion towards strangers and loved-ones alike held greater significance to me than my social status, my financial standing or my religious affiliations.

But all those ideals had come crashing down at that moment. I was a saint and a crusader for humanity until it suited me, until I came face to face with the murky predicaments of human existence in a way that affected someone close to me. My kindness, when stripped down to its roots, was nothing but a by-product of my privilege. I was an imposter, a hypocrite. In the face of adversity, I had emerged a blood-sucking monster from behind a mask of benevolence. In the desperation to save my own husband, another dead man was only a freed-up ICU bed to me and nothing more.

I was walking the path many did that terrible summer—cutting lines in order to get oxygen cylinders refuelled for their gasping loved ones, paying exorbitant prices for critical medicines in short supply, or using high profile connections to get a slot for their loved ones at the cremation ground while the other dead bodies rotted on the sidewalks. A lot of us stand guilty, in one way or the other, of having crossed the line, the threshold of our inherent humanity.

The in-charge's words did not deter me. After hours of persistence and multiple follow ups, Abhinav was at last ready to be moved. A sense of relief washed over me knowing that he will now be given the best available treatment and access to the most advanced machines in the hospital. "Nothing could possibly happen to him here," I reassured myself.

However, as we wheeled him through the ICU doors, the loud and relentless beeping of the machines, the harsh lights and the nervous movements of the nurses made my head spin. I studied the patients occupying the beds on either side of this endless room. Many appeared to be in their middle age or older. Some were labouring to breathe through their masks, while others lay unconscious. A few beds were hidden behind drawn curtains. It was only later that I learned that those people were either on life support or even already dead.

My heart sank.

It seemed incredibly unfair for Abhinav to be in a room full of people who had all already lived significant portions of their lives. He was much younger than most of them, at least by two decades if not more. He still had so many experiences to live through in the long life that awaited him outside these treacherous doors.

I wanted to scream at the top of my lungs, "This is unfair! He doesn't belong here! We just got married, HOW IS THIS HAPPENING!" to ensure that everyone in that room—doctors, nurses, patients—could see it as the glaring aberration that it was.

As if they held any power to change any of it at all.

As the nurses helped Abhinav settle in his new bed, the third one in the same night, I could sense his spirits sinking. He muttered repeatedly, "I know I am going down the rabbit hole, I know I am not coming alive out of this."

Dread gripped me at his words, but I tried my best to console him, assuring him, "Nothing will happen to you here, you are in intensive care. You will recover very soon. I promise." I didn't say it merely to calm his nerves. I uttered those words with wholehearted conviction, because that is what I truly believed as well.

Nothing could happen to Abhinav.

9

Other Stories from the ICU

One major downside of admitting Abhinav to the ICU was that I couldn't stay by his side at all times, and it made me anxious. Unlike the ward, the ICU had strict restrictions on visitations. As a result, I ended up spending several nights in the waiting hall, where I witnessed many other stories unfolding around me. I was not the only person whose life was hanging by a thread, clung to a loved one admitted inside the ICU.

A woman in her late forties was stationed in the waiting area, flanked by her two teenage children, clutching onto a couple of bags. Spotting me sitting alone, she inched towards me and began sharing. "My husband is inside. He has been on the ventilator for ten days now. We don't have any insurance, our savings are depleting with each passing day."

She continued in the same breath, " I saw when they were taking your husband in. He was fully conscious. Not like my husband, he was completely unconscious when we brought him here."

She paused briefly, then added, "Your husband should be okay soon, he seems fine." To be polite, I responded, "Your husband will recover as well, don't worry," although I didn't have the faintest idea about his condition.

Her teenage daughter was an endless lament of regret and anxiety. "We should have taken Papa to a different hospital. The doctors here aren't good. In fact, we shouldn't have taken Papa to a hospital at all." I wanted to nod in agreement. The same thought had been bugging me for days now.

For the nights that she was there, when not soothing her agitated children, she would continuously run a string of beads through her fingers and chant some mantras. Seeing her do that, I felt compelled to pray for Abhinav's well-being as well. I didn't know any mantras by heart, so I would play the Hanuman Chalisa on my phone and listen to it on repeat through headphones.

On that first night, there was also a much older man, in his late sixties, who was pacing back and forth across the ICU doors. His wife was inside, and he had hired a private nurse to tend to her needs along with the hospital staff. Many had opted for private nurses during the time to ensure their ailing family members received care while shielding themselves from the virus. The next morning, when that nurse emerged from the ICU, she announced, "She is eating properly. She finished both the chapatis. The doctor says that she is out of danger and they will soon move her to a regular ward." His face lit up at the news.

I wondered which of the two narratives Abhinav's story would follow, all the while desperately hoping for the second one.

On the third night I was there, a middle-aged man, covered in a full-body PPE suit, dashed out of the ICU, visibly distraught and in tears. The woman with the teenage kids leaned over to me and whispered, "His mother is being put on a ventilator. He was called in to say his last goodbyes."

That sinking feeling again. There was tragedy unravelling all around me, live, as I watched.

On the night he was admitted to the ICU, Abhinav continued to text me with whatever energy he had left in him. He was in constant discomfort. Earlier, the discomfort arose only from the excessive effort required for breathing, but now, the perennial clamour of the ICU added to it. Unlike the relative peace of the ward, the ICU was in constant and complete chaos. Lights were always on, and there was disconcerting noise at all hours from the rushed movements of the staff and the beeping of machines attached to more than a dozen patients. Sleep eluded him. I made a note to get him a pair of earplugs and an eye mask the next day.

When the doctor arrived the following morning, I couldn't hold back my frustration from the fatigue of the sleepless night before. I asked him point blank, the one question that had been lingering unspoken in all our minds: "What are his chances?"

Mom and Papa had also arrived by that time.

The doctor paused briefly before responding, "There is always a chance. There is always hope. We should not lose hope yet," and left. Mom, reassured by his response, attempted to lift my spirits, "See, even the doctor believes he'll be fine! You're worrying too much. Abhinav will start recovering soon."

I chose not to shatter her hopes. But, I knew deep within my heart that the doctor's words were a white lie; that he was merely trying to avoid giving us a real answer because he knew what was to come. He had hesitated; his eyes hadn't met mine. Our fatigued yet hopeful faces had distressed him in some way, and he had decided at that moment that he didn't want to be the bearer of the most terrible news there could be. I had seen that face before; I recognised it too well.

When I was not running from one doctor to another, or from the hospital to home and back, I would take brief breaks to invigorate myself. I would give myself a forced serotonin boost by conjuring a fairy tale ending to all of it: Abhinav is finally discharged from the hospital, panting but slowly ascending the stairs of our Delhi residence. I have decorated our living room with a huge "Welcome Back" sign, and he is cutting a cake that says "Defeated COVID." We have meticulously disinfected the entire house to ensure he doesn't catch any infections during his recovery. I have taken a month-long break from work to look after him full-time. I can once again lay my head on his chest and be reunited with the familiar rhythm of his heart. As I slowly nurture him back to health, our bond grows deeper in the aftermath of this adversity.

Even as the situation grew worse by the minute, I refused to imagine the worst. Even while tumbling through a downward spiral, my mind, in an attempt to protect itself from total collapse and keep my body going, kept me deluded with this imaginary, happily-ever-after ending. Every next moment seemed like the moment of redemption. Every dawn seemed like the promise of a new day when recovery would begin. Every next minute seemed like the one when Abhinav would magically pull out of the worst of this affliction.

It simply *couldn't* end any other way.

While I enveloped myself in the embrace of this false hope, I remained oblivious to the clues that fate had been leaving all around. I had looked the other way when the living room clock—which Abhinav and I had bought together for our new house—had repeatedly stopped working. Despite getting it repaired multiple times and replacing its batteries, it would inexplicably stop every few days. I kept reminding myself to discard it, knowing well that a broken clock was a bad omen, but I kept forgetting about it. I had looked the other way when several "Cremation Ground" locations kept popping up on Google Maps navigation as Papa drove us to fetch medicines for Abhinav. For a brief moment, my heart did skip a beat, but I quickly dispelled those thoughts as foolish. I had looked the other way when the kurta that Abhinav's aunt had unwittingly offered me to change into, on the morning of Abhinav's death, was entirely devoid of colour. It was a muted beige, as if something in the universe was nudging her hand, signalling to her that I was going to be widowed in an hour.

There were signs everywhere, as my life was crumbling in the face of irony, but I was determined to look the other way and coerce myself into fantasising about a reality that was never going to be.

10

My Worst Fears Coming True

By May 21, 2021, Abhinav was being pumped a staggering thirty litres of oxygen at a time, fifteen of which were delivered through a mouth mask and fifteen through two thin tubes inserted into his nostrils. But despite this increased oxygen support, his saturation levels were dropping below 70%. The doctors continued to avoid our questions about what was happening and what needed to be done next. Meanwhile, the nurses were attempting to get Abhinav to use the BiPAP machine, but he remained unable to endure it.

The limited visitation hours in the ICU afforded me very little time with him. I had to plead with the nurses to let me in, and moments after letting me inside, they would start insisting that I leave. In whatever little precious time I got with him, I grew increasingly despondent at his diminishing hope, which was evident as he reiterated, "I am going down a rabbit hole! I am not coming out of it alive!"

He was a bit disoriented and noticeably infuriated, and he had every right to be. A mere fifteen days ago, he was planning his next vacation, exercising regularly to better his health, planning to host a gathering of friends once COVID-19 subsided, even contemplating prospects of parenthood in a year or two. Through all of these aspirations, both trivial and monumental, he was planning for the rest of his life that stretched ahead of him. And suddenly, with a tragic twist of fate, he found himself grappling, with every laboured breath that he took, for mere survival.

The same day, around 10 pm, I got access to a fresh set of Abhinav's test results. By now, I had become adept at deciphering the numbers, initials, acronyms, percentages. To my continued dismay, I saw no hope in any one of them. Disheartened, I still took pictures of all the pages and the X-ray films and shared it with everyone.

Within moments, my phone began to ring. It was Dr. Pawan, a neighbour of Abhinav's parents, whom we were consulting on Abhinav's case for the past few days. Although he wasn't affiliated with the hospital where Abhinav was admitted, he was overseeing Abhinav's treatment along with the in-hospital doctors. There was an unmistakable panic and sense of urgency in his voice. "These reports are not looking good at all. Abhinav is in real danger of collapsing anytime! We need to put him on a ventilator immediately. I am coming over right away."

My heart started pounding, threatening to burst out of my chest. The fragile bouts of hope that were keeping me going until now almost immediately began abandoning me. As I awaited Dr. Pawan's arrival, I found myself already beginning to grieve the life that I had built with Abhinav, while he was still 'alive'. Though I tried to fight the feeling, a profound sense of loss gripped me and crippled my body.

I began to imagine a future devoid of him. A future bereft of any direction, any sense of belonging—another trauma mounted on to the pile of traumas that I had accumulated over the last three decades, that I had barely managed to survive. How will I possibly live through this one? Every cell in my body reverberated with this question. I imagined Abhinav dead for the first time, and the feeling crushed me into a million little pieces.

As hope slipped through my fingers, a raging frustration began to brew vehemently inside of me. I was angry at the fact that we had ended up here. I was angry that after spending seven years, painstakingly trying to pick up the pieces of my life that were shattered after my father's death, I had somehow managed to land in the same harrowing circumstances again. I was, once again, standing at the doorstep of another imminent tragedy, another trauma ready to tear me apart. I was standing outside another ICU trying to save another man who meant the world to me, and failing terribly at it. The memories of my father's death and the painful events leading up to it were fresh in my mind again. It was déjà vu of the most devastating kind.

Standing frozen in the waiting area, I felt terribly alone once again, much like I had felt seven years ago. Of course, I did have Mom and Papa this time around, whose hearts were bleeding as much as mine. They relied on their faith in their gods and continued to pray fervently to their gallery of Hindu deities. I, on the other hand, relied on medical science and the doctors overseeing

Abhinav's treatment. Both of our faiths would fail us soon; we could sense it, but we couldn't get ourselves to accept that just yet.

I found myself in a tumultuous storm of emotions. One moment, my exhausted body wanted to give up and relinquish this losing battle to someone else more competent. The very next moment, this desire would be quickly replaced by a fear of surrendering control. I couldn't trust anyone else to see this mission through with the same ferocity that I did.

Between the ebbs and the flow of my sanity, I somehow managed to keep myself together. I had to stand strong for my husband. Tears threatened to breach the dam of my resolve, but I staunchly held them back. I kept coercing myself into believing that all was not lost yet. Maybe, maybe there was still a chance that a miracle would reverse the flow of these tragic events.

At around 11:00 pm, Dr. Pawan arrived. He was accompanied by three other doctors who he had brought together to take a "decision" on Abhinav. The group included Abhinav's doctor from the hospital, a pulmonologist and an anaesthetist, the only woman among them. They all rushed directly to the ICU and instructed me to wait outside. My agony mounted with each passing moment that they were inside and I was not in the know.

Another fifteen minutes passed, and I was summoned back into the ICU. Inside, I was met with the sight of all four doctors standing in a line formation, their shoulders nearly touching, their hands clasped in front of them. They did it in unison, almost as a reflex reaction to my presence. It was like a well-coordinated doomsday choreography, taught to them in medical school in a course called "How to Approach the Family of a Terminally Ill Patient." They all stood close to the ICU door, far from Abhinav's bed.

I quickly studied the group before me. They were all middle-aged, with prominent patches of grey visible in their hair. Dr. Pawan seemed to be the youngest of them all. As they stood, they towered over me, and I felt small. I could barely muster the courage to look them in the eye, but I had to; I needed my answers.

Abhinav's attending doctor was the first one to talk. "Is there someone else we can speak to?" Perhaps he was deceived by my stature and thought, "What will this five feet zero inches of a woman decide? What if she is unable to handle what we are about to say?"

"His parents are on the way but for now it is just me, his wife," I responded.

He let out a brief sigh and began explaining, "Abhinav's situation is extremely critical. We need to put him on a ventilator. We will need you to sign a No Objection Certificate to give us permission to do that." He paused for a moment and added, "But before you make that decision, you should know what it means to put him on a ventilator."

I had already Googled what it meant, but I heard him out anyway. "A ventilator, or life support, is the last resort measure to save a person whose vital organs are rapidly failing. Typically, there is a survival rate of 50% or less once a person is placed on a ventilator. Even if the patient survives, the highly intrusive nature of the device can lead to irreversible damage to the body."

Dr. Pawan added, "You must understand how delicate Abhinav's situation is. There is a possibility of losing him *while* we are moving him to the ventilator. Once he is intubated, we need to perform some additional procedures on him. For those, too, we will require your consent. Each procedure we perform from now on has a certain level of risk associated with it. With each procedure, he will have a 30-40% chance of survival."

I wanted to protest the discrepancy in their numbers. "But the other doctor said 50% chance of survival earlier!" Instead, I simply nodded as I absorbed all of that information. The probability of Abhinav's survival was diminishing with every second we spent in the ICU.

So this was it. This was how it was all supposed to end.

In a matter of moments, Abhinav would be anaesthetized, a big plastic tube would be shoved inside his body and a machine would take control of him. He would cease to be the Abhinav I knew and loved.

"Should we proceed, then?" Abhinav's doctor inquired while I was trying to process all I had just heard.

"Don't ask me this. He is all I have!" I wanted to scream at him. "Don't snatch him away from me. I won't survive without him!"

Instead, I glanced at Dr. Pawan, silently seeking his guidance. He responded with a nod; we had no other choice but to proceed. Time was of the essence and we couldn't afford to lose any more of it.

I asked for a moment from the doctors. I had to consult with Mom and Papa. I didn't want to carry the weight of this decision alone. I knew they didn't know any better than me, but I had to hear it from them. Papa answered his phone and said dejectedly, "Whatever Dr. Pawan says, we will go with that."

Once I signed the NOC, they asked me to leave the room. I found myself thinking, "30-40% chances of survival. Those are still pretty good odds. Abhinav can still make it." Even then, I wasn't able to let go of hope entirely. I was ready to believe that a million-to-one odds were still good enough odds in our favour. The heart wanted to see the end it wanted to see—a last-minute escape from fate, a magical recovery, the going back to life as it was.

The nurses and doctors flung into action to intubate Abhinav. After twenty minutes or so, Dr. Pawan came out of the ICU.

11

One Last Time

"You should come inside and speak with Abhinav once," Dr. Pawan said to me gently. He didn't say anything else, but I understood from the tone of his voice that this could very well be the last time that I'd get to talk to Abhinav.

As I struggled to restrain the tears of utter disbelief of where life had brought us so soon in our journey together, I quickly began to gather my thoughts. What should I say to him that would sum up all that he meant to me? What should I say to him that would make up for all the love that I was yet to share with him in the decades to come? What should I say to him to make up for the lifetime of togetherness that was being snatched away from us? What should I say to him to make up for all the life that he was never going to experience? What should I say to him to make up for *everything*?!

Every fibre of my being wanted to scream, "Abhinav, I will die without you!" I wanted to sink to my knees and plead to him with folded hands, "Don't leave me! I can't imagine a second of my life without you!" I wanted to hold him accountable for abandoning me like this, "You were supposed to save me! You promised!" I wanted to say all of that and so much more, but I suppressed those thoughts along with the tears. Gathering myself, I tried to clear my mind. It was not the time to go berserk, I must infuse in Abhinav and his body the strength to fight longer, fight harder.

I walked towards him. Heavy brown curtains now veiled his bed. As I parted the curtains, I found that I was not alone with him. Five or six nurses, a mix of men and women, surrounded his bed. Some fiddled with the devices and tubes that were already tethered to his body, others were holding new devices, perhaps required for intubation. Their actions momentarily paused, they looked at me expectantly as they waited for me to finish the "talking", so that they could get on with the task at hand.

I made space for myself amidst the group to get a view of my husband; he was struggling to breathe and appeared to be gradually drifting into unconsciousness. My eyes instinctually located the monitors to get a glimpse of the parameter that I had been tracking every few hours, for the last fifteen days now—his oxygen saturation. The number was dipping with each passing second—70%, 65%, 68%, 60%...

I took his right hand into mine and stroked it gently, hoping it would relieve some of his pain. He gave me a laboured glance, then shut his eyes. More nurses and doctors joined us around the already crowded bed. I longed for a moment to speak to my husband in private, but I also understood that there was no time left to indulge in that. I began to speak, my voice quivering but determined, "Babe, nothing is going to happen. We won't let anything happen to you. The medical team is about to conduct another procedure, and you may lose consciousness briefly. But you will be back on your feet in no time. Once you recover and return home, we will do whatever you say. We will take time off, just like you wanted—no office, no house work. We will go for a nice relaxing vacation. And that drone you've always wanted? I'm all in for that."

He interrupted me, his breathing strained. "And...let's not forget, we will both get a personal trainer, a top-notch one, and start working out seriously."

His statement momentarily caught me off guard, but soon after a surge of pride washed over me. He hadn't surrendered to despair; hope was still alive within him.

Perhaps he thought that his recovery would follow the same trajectory as his first roommate's in the hospital—the twenty-something man from the ward who had been unconscious for a few days before he had started regaining strength and was discharged soon after. Or perhaps it was just his indomitable spirit that was determined to keep fighting.

I continued to whisper in his ears—hope of the most mundane things of life, while he stood at the edge of it. "Mom will make your favourite pav bhaji for you, once you are back. We will have a big celebration..." and so on and so forth.

Dr. Pawan was now signalling to me—it was time. Abhinav's oxygen was crashing rapidly. I hurriedly squeezed his hand and said, for the last time, "Remember, I love you with all my heart."

Something that we would casually say to each other every day, countless times a day. When he would hand me a breakfast plate, "I love you"; when we would finish talking to each other on the phone, "I love you"; when he would plant a kiss on my forehead while I was working, "I love you." A prompt "I love you too" would always follow intuitively. Something that was so ingrained that it was a reflex action of my everyday interaction with him, that something had become absolutely vital to assert in that moment.

I couldn't stop the tears anymore.

By now, Abhinav's eyes were slowly closing and his body was beginning to tilt the other way, away from me. He was in way too much pain to keep up with what I was saying. Nonetheless, he responded, "I love you too," feebly.

But that would not suffice, not at this moment.

I squeezed his hand firmly and demanded that he say it to me like he meant it. "Abhinav, look at me and say it!" I chided him. I wanted him to say it to me in the way he had said it to me for the very first time. I wanted him to say it to me in a way that could last me a lifetime. I struggled to drown out all the distractions around us—the beeping of machines, the bustling noises, the general commotion of the ICU—to etch his voice and those words on to the deepest recesses of my heart so as to never forget what we had.

To never forget what we could be in the time we had, and to never forget what we couldn't be in eternity.

He opened his eyes as much as his fragile body could allow, his gaze locking onto mine. With a fleeting smile gracing his lips, he murmured, "I love you too," and then drifted away again. I finally let go of his hand and ran outside, bursting into a flood of tears that felt like it would last forever and run me dry.

Deep-rooted sorrow grips my soul every time I let myself wonder about the thoughts that must be swirling in Abhinav's mind at the time. What does a young man, finding himself facing imminent death and a wailing wife, think about? Was he aware that the translucent green tube that the nurse had just pulled out from the sterile plastic bag was going to be forced inside his throat? Was he aware that at that moment, he merely held a 30% chance of survival?

How much did his body hurt? Did it hurt as much as when I had fractured my foot and felt a pain so searing run through my leg that I forgot to breathe for minutes on end, or was it a million times worse than that? How suffocated did he feel breathing at 65% oxygen? Was it the same as when I trekked to 18,000 feet and found myself gasping for air, or was it a million times worse than that? How did it feel to be so close to death? Was it as dreadful, as terrifying as the feeling when an aeroplane suddenly plummets several kilometres mid-air during turbulence, or was it a million times worse than that?

A year-and-a-half into his death, I lie awake on several nights, agitated and wailing, thinking about the excruciating pain that his body must have endured, but also about the agonising thoughts that must have plagued his mind— the anguish of the laboured breathing, the bigger anguish of life's hopes and aspirations crashing around him.

In my more logical moments, I am more aware of the fact that he is not here anymore, suffering as he was that day. I know he is more at peace than I will ever be as I continue to live. I know that he has vanished from the face of earth, and with him, all the pain that existed on that day has vanished as well. The recognition of this truth should bring me some reprieve, but strangely enough, it doesn't. That moment and that feeling stay permanently, like a throbbing stab wound to the heart.

***

About thirty minutes later, I was handed Abhinav's belongings—primarily his phone, which had been keeping him busy over the last few days—along with the phone's charger, his ear buds and his sleeping mask. I clutched those items in my hands, staring at them blankly. I signed a few other NOCs to authorise some other procedures that night.

By that time, Mom and Papa had also arrived. We huddled around Dr. Pawan as he explained to us, "The virus is rapidly damaging all his vital organs. But we do have various instruments, procedures and medications on standby in case any of his organs suffer damage to the point of absolute failure. Should his lungs falter even with life support, we can consider putting him on a device called ECMO that will help him breathe externally. In the event of a drastic drop in his blood pressure, we have medication that can be added to his bloodstream to keep it pumping. If his kidneys get affected and stop functioning, we will start him on dialysis."

It appeared that the doctors had a fool-proof plan in place for anything and everything that could possibly go wrong, and I could feel my face light up, albeit only slightly.

Maybe there was still a chance.

What I didn't understand then was that the human body could still simply give up, despite getting all the necessary attention. What I didn't comprehend was that life support was not a no-fail solution. What I couldn't grasp at the time was that even with access to all that modern technology, a person could still, just, die.

It was two days after he was moved to the ventilator that Abhinav suffered a septic shock. His blood pressure had crashed.

Part III

Days After

12

The Angst, the Anger and the Agony

For you to feel absolutely nothing at last, you must feel absolutely everything at first.

The initial days after Abhinav's death are blurry now, but I distinctly remember thinking that I would not survive it. I felt a constant stabbing pain inside my chest so intense I thought my body was shutting down. An unrelenting jitter had taken over me, as if I was a drug addict who had been forced to go cold turkey, the sudden shock making me tremble with withdrawal.

I needed Abhinav desperately; I needed him to hold me still and to warm my cold, shivering body. It was him and only him who could take away the pain he had inflicted upon me. I remember the incredulous reaction my body would have to anyone attempting to touch me, hug me, stroke my arms to console me—it would instinctively pull itself away from them. *They* were not the comfort it wanted.

I confined myself to a bedroom in Mom and Papa's home, crying through the day. At night, I couldn't get myself to sleep. I would lie awake all night, crying, yearning for his warmth, a sensation that had so abruptly abandoned me. Eventually, my sobs would lull me into an uneasy sleep, my body curled onto one side. I would wake up finding my right hand clutching the left, tightly, the fingers of the two hands crisscrossing each other, almost as if my body was trying create the illusion that he was still there, holding me.

I was growing ever more insane with each passing hour.

Each nightmare I had in those days followed an almost similar narrative: Abhinav desperately trying to distance himself from me. I would see him trying to escape from our wedding at the last minute while I ran after him in my heavy, blinging lehenga; a stream of tears streaking down my cheeks and smearing my kajal along with it. In another such nightmare, I would see him breaking up with me because he was relocating to another city for work. However, the most tormenting nightmares were those where I would find myself uncovering that he had been fabricating his death all this time. He was doing it to get rid of me, because he was fed up with my emotionally anxious self and had found someone more mentally stable.

No matter what the scene was, it would invariably end the same way. I would eventually catch hold of him and confront him, sobbing hysterically, "Why are you running away from me? Why don't you want to be with me anymore? Why don't you love me anymore???" He would remain unresponsive, my pleas to reconsider our relationship falling on deaf ears. He would just stand there, disgusted with me, his body rigid as a stone, his gaze averted, while I continued to beg.

While these horrifying nightmares plagued my nights; during the day, I would immerse myself in the illusion that nothing had changed, that Abhinav was still very much alive, just not with me right then. I would imagine him self-isolating in the apartment above, much like when Papa, Mom and I had contracted the virus.

I imagined him waiting for me on the other side of the meshed door, adorning the striking blue polo t-shirt that he looked so handsome in. I imagined his face like that, slightly obscured by the mesh and the mask he wore, but whose silhouette asserted his presence. With a racing heart, I'd dash to the door, longing for a final glance of him, only to be met with disappointment.

***

I felt a tumultuous rage that would culminate into regular, almost hourly, psychotic explosions. There was enough fury in me to burn the entire world down to ashes. I was furious at the universe that robbed Abhinav of his life. I was furious at the dozens of relatives who showed up after his death, who hadn't shown up when he was still alive. I wanted to unleash all that fury on them, "Where were you when we were trying to save him? What have you come to do now?" I was furious at everyone who continued to live a seemingly mundane life, who didn't know the devastation of death as yet. I was furious at Abhinav's parents for not being furious enough. I was furious at myself for being naive enough to believe that I could alter my fate.

I simmered with fury at all the people who had not succumbed to COVID-19 yet.

As the virus continued to run amok, several crowdsourcing platforms emerged, allowing those in need to raise funds for their loved ones in critical condition. In the days after Abhinav's death, I found myself scrolling through these fundraisers, tracking which of them had been closed, which of them had now become "in memory of so and so" instead of "to save so and so."

Although I had donated to some of these fundraisers while Abhinav was in the hospital, I didn't press the "Donate Now" button anymore. Instead, I now desperately wished for all those people to meet the same fate as my husband. No one should escape the fury of COVID-19 if he couldn't. I wanted the entire human race to burn in the same flames of agony that I burned in.

Above all, I was furious at Abhinav.

Why did he have to come into my life if he was going to leave me so soon after? In my own narcissistic way, I believed it was so much easier for him to be dead, and that death had warranted him a convenient escape from the soul-crushing pain that I was left with.

I desperately started scouring through his belongings—his phone, his social media accounts, his hard drives, even his diary—in a hopeless attempt to find something that would make me despise him, or to uncover an ugly truth that would make it easier for me to let go of him. I wasn't particularly sure about what I was really trying to look for. Perhaps I wanted to unearth a hint of betrayal that would shatter my heart and, maybe, also alleviate my pain. I wanted to stumble upon something that would allow me to feel something else, something more or something less—just not this.

I wondered if he had been flirting with other women, or was venting about me to his friends. Or even worse, that perhaps he didn't love me in the all-consuming way I thought he did. In a strange, masochistic tradition, I wished some, or all, of it to be true.

I flipped through the pages of the journal that I had gifted him on Valentine's Day, a couple of months back. The journal had a unique question on each page for each of the 365 days of the year with a small space to record answers for the same question for five consecutive years. The questions ranged from lighthearted prompts like, "Who is the craziest person you know?", "Who are you living with right now?" to more introspective ones like "What do you aspire to be?" I had purchased two copies of it, one for me, one for him, excited to see how our lives would unfold over the next five years and how our responses would change over time.

I turned through the pages, apprehensive of what I might discover about him. To my relief, the diary was a genuine reflection of Abhinav's true self. It was speckled with his desire to travel more, notes about cherished moments with friends, endearing mentions of his "wife" and other silly responses that made me smile through my tears.

But then, somewhere between the pages, there was a question, "Whom do you confide your deepest secrets to?" To which he had said, "Nobody. Nobody truly knows what is going on in my mind." That answer, etched in his handwriting, broke my heart. I felt as if I had been blindsided, especially since I had responded with a clear and resounding "Abhinav" to the same question. Because that was my truth—he knew about all my anxieties, my fears, my dilemmas and I had believed that I knew all about him as well.

His answer ignited a storm of doubts in my mind, that was already too fragile and suffering—What else did I not know about him? Was he really happy with me in the way that I thought he was? Did we really have what I thought we had or was it all a fabrication of my naive soul?

Was I just a fool?

A few days later, while browsing through the archives of his hard drive, I stumbled upon a five-year-old photograph featuring a woman who might have been an ex-girlfriend. Perhaps it was something that was just *there*, forgotten and buried in the digital clutter. Perhaps he hadn't looked at it in years. Nonetheless, I was infuriated. Why did he still have it? Am I mourning a man who never truly loved me? The thought began to haunt me day and night.

Vulnerable like I had never been before, every new piece of his past that I discovered seemed like a big question mark on our relationship. Every little detail that deviated, even if slightly, from the narrative that I had built about us, seemed like a profound deceit. In just a few days after his passing, a multitude of questions had sprung within me, and I desperately wanted to find him and confront him with those.

After the storm of suspicion and betrayal would wear me out, my emotional pendulum would swing towards abject dejection, thinking how Abhinav was now, for all intents and purposes, frozen in time; how he would never get to be a year older than thirty-three, how I would never see him to be forty or sixty or eighty; how it was now left to my imagination to fabricate an aged version of him as I pass through the different stages of my life; to imagine him as a middle-aged man, his belly protruding, patches of grey in his hair; to imagine him as a 60 year old, wearing a wrinkled but content smile of a life well lived. Perhaps he would have begun resembling Papa as he aged; or perhaps not—I guess I will never know. Abhinav had been deprived of all of this, and the realisation tore me apart.

I thought it would kill me. I knew this was it. I couldn't possibly survive this. If this wasn't going to push me over the edge and wrench my soul out of my body, then what would? Why was I still alive?

I wanted something or someone to kill me, to end this misery for me, once and for all. To stab me in the chest with a sharp knife, or shoot me with a bullet, shattering my skull into pieces, or simply push me off the edge of a towering skyscraper, not leaving me the slightest chance of survival.

I didn't *want* to survive this.

13

The Panicked Attempt to Save Myself

I had to put an end to this torment; I couldn't possibly continue like this. I didn't trust those around me to help me navigate a problem that felt so unique to me. So in my desperation, I turned to Google for answers. I wanted to see if I could instead rely on the collective knowledge of the universe to guide me out of this darkness that was slowly sucking the life out of me but refused to kill me in entirety.

I frantically typed in the myriad questions that agonised me: "Why did my husband die at thirty-three?" "How do I live after my husband's death?" "What is the easiest way to kill myself?" "Will I ever get over my grief?" "Why do some people die young?" "Can you change your destiny?" "Why does my life keep getting fucked over and over again???"

To my dismay, all I found was standard textbook information repeated across websites. Most articles listed and explained the same five stages of grief, theorised by Elisabeth Kübler-Ross in 1969: denial, anger, bargaining, depression and acceptance. The articles added that these stages were not always experienced linearly. One could experience multiple stages at the same time, could skip certain stages or could remain stuck on one stage for an extended period.

But that was all. That's where the articles would always stop.

I found solace in the fact that I understood every bit of what they were saying, relating deeply with the emotional upheaval that the 'anger' and 'denial' phases caused. However, what continued to frustrate me was that they didn't tell me how to speed up these phases—how to end this cycle of pain, how to stop the agony that I was grappling with.

I continued my search. Several attempts later, I landed on some websites that shared succinct lists of "to-dos" to combat grief. These "to-dos" mostly revolved around the following five themes:

1. Keep yourself hydrated

2. Surround yourself with family and friends

3. Look towards God to guide you

4. Rekindle your interest in your hobbies

5. Exercise

I was flummoxed. Didn't these writers know that my entire existence was hanging by a thread? Did they really believe that rekindling a hobby would save me from this profound crisis? At a time when I was struggling to get out of bed, how did they expect me to start exercising?

Some of those articles did strike me as absurd in those initial days of grieving. They had to be, I thought, the attempts of those distant observers of grief who had never experienced as heartbreaking a loss as mine and couldn't possibly be the advice of someone who had actually been through it.

In the course of my online quest, I also, inadvertently, landed upon a few alarming studies on the death of a partner. I came across the "widowhood effect" which said, "... individuals whose spouses pass away stand a 66% increased chance of dying within the initial three months following their spouse's demise." I didn't really pause to read the finer details of the study, but I began to believe in the possibility of it happening. I had no trouble imagining how a person's body could crumble under the weight of the trauma that ensued after a partner's death; the trauma that I now found myself face-to-face with.

I really did feel like I could die, that I could become a part of that 66%. And I was prepared for it; death certainly seemed like the easiest way out of my misery.

Soon, I gave up on the internet and got myself some books.

I knew that Sheryl Sandberg, the former COO of Facebook, had penned a book called *Option B* after the sudden death of her husband at the age of 47.

I was filled with hope when I picked it up. Surely, someone as intelligent and accomplished as her would have the answers.

The book is, indeed, beautiful, and I resonated with a lot of the raw, painful feelings that she felt and wrote eloquently about; but my fundamental questions still remained unanswered.

I kept looking, and I stumbled upon quite a few books on death and grief. It included *The Year of Magical Thinking* by Joan Didion, *A Grief Observed* by C.S. Lewis, *Tuesdays With Morrie* by Mitch Albom and others. I read them all and I read more, but none of it seemed to help.

My thirst for answers was unquenched, and my body was trembling in the aftermath of Abhinav's loss. I was enraged and furious at not being able to contain my misery, for not being able to find a way out of this hell.

What I was failing to comprehend at the time was that I couldn't simply escape this feeling with a snap of my fingers. My anguish was the direct result of my profound love for Abhinav. The incessant wailing, the terrifying nightmares, the simmering anxiety, were all manifestations of that once delightful love.

I had to go through this insidious suffering to pay the price for placing him at the centre of my universe; I had to feel this pain deep within my bones until it either consumed me entirely or released its grip on me.

I had to go through it to get anywhere at all

14

"Be Strong"

Even in the middle of a sea of people, grief feels like a lifetime sentence to solitary confinement.

When the very foundation of your world collapses, you begin to despise everyone else whose worlds remain intact. They come across as vicious as they go on with their mundane lives. Those who do momentarily pause to grieve with you end up saying the wrong things, and for you, that's enough to push them away. Perhaps everything anyone says seems wrong in the early days of grief.

I continued to stay with Abhinav's parents for the first two months after his death. Mom and Papa insisted that I don't leave for Gurgaon immediately after. Looking back, it was a wise decision. If it wasn't for them, I would have just wasted away, like a melancholic Victorian, drowned in my own misery, without feeling the need to eat, drink or bathe.

At the time, however, I remember feeling trapped. I felt stifled by their constant need to console me; angry, even. They would get agitated at the slightest display of sadness from me. Whether it was my quiet sniffling in my room or my hysterical outbursts for all to see, they would rush to pacify me.

As they tried to shield me from my sorrow, they grieved the death of their son in their own way. They did it more subtly, weeping behind closed doors and sobbing at night, without making a sound. They did it while continuing to maintain the humdrum of a normal household. Mom ensured that the kitchen was functional and that everyone was well-fed. Papa took charge of settling outstanding hospital and pharmacy bills. They were both busy catering to the many guests who would show up at the house to commiserate while I languished in my room. Unlike me, they neither had the luxury nor the temperament to give up on their obligations and give in to the weight of their grief.

Perhaps they believed that the more civilised and acceptable approach to grief dictates that grieving should be in moderation, that it should not be all-consuming. You cry, but you cry when no one is looking. You sniffle and not howl. You carry on with the motions of your regular life. You smile and put on a brave face when visitors show up. Because you should be dignified even in the face of a world-shattering event. Because, God forbid, if you somehow end up revealing your raw, vulnerable self, you end up breaking the implied social contract of keeping your emotions repressed and not making society uncomfortable.

Several people showed up after the first few days of mourning, as they always do. It felt as though they had come to survey the debris and ruins of the tsunami that had just passed through.

"Be strong," they said, not knowing the tremendous amount of strength that was needed to simply continue to draw breath. "God needed him more than we did," they said, failing to understand how desperately *we* needed him. "Time will heal," they said, not knowing that time now felt endless, interminable, forever-tormenting.

In their platitudes, I couldn't find a drop of empathy or rationale. All I saw was pity and a sense of otherness towards our tragedy.

Then there were the malicious comments that questioned the very foundation of my relationship with Abhinav. First, there were the "at leasts": "At least you are young, you will find someone else," "At least you don't have children, that would have made it difficult to find another husband," "At least you have a job."

Then there was the genuine perplexity at the extent of my grief, "But you were both married for just over a year, how come you are so attached to him? How can it affect you so much?"

"Move on," they said to my face.

Deeply hurt and vulnerable, I tried to explain and convince them, those that simply didn't understand my loss, "But we were dating for two years before that!" "But he was my husband!" "But I loved him deeply. I really did!!!"

This astonishment at my grief made me wonder how many years were sufficient to justify a widow's hysteria—would five years have better rationalised my anguish, or did we have to be together for at least ten years for people to stop questioning my grief? Later, I encountered another COVID-19 widow who had been married for a mere five months before she lost her husband. I wondered if that made it easier for her to "move on."

The "at leasts" left me wondering which category of widows were better off. Those with children could argue that the childless widows had it easier. Conversely, the childless widows could assert that they were worse off because without kids, there was no continuity to their husband's legacy and no clear purpose to their own lives. The young widows felt that their loss was premature, and the older ones, too, believed that it was too soon for them. As much as I tried to solve this conundrum, there appeared to be no definitive criteria, timeframe or circumstance which would make losing a partner less devastating.

What I did realise was how easy it was for everyone to rationalise my pain. While our own challenges and dilemmas are always humongous and insufferable, we are very swift in trivialising the suffering of others into fairly resolvable problems. We are crude robots with a primitive understanding of the human psyche when it comes to the complexities of misery of others—a dead husband meant "get a new one." "How could it be so difficult for her to resolve this? What was all this hue and cry about?"

A part of me chalked it down to age. The older generation were moulded in certain ways of how they thought about death, and all they could offer were the age-old consolations that they had heard and used all their lives.

So I turned to the young, hoping they would at least attempt to understand how catastrophic it might be for someone their age to go through what I was going through. Unfortunately, with the exception of a few, I was met with a whole lot of disappointment again.

A close friend of mine attempted to console me, "You are strong. You dealt with your father's death with such strength. You will get over this as well." She believed her words would help me persevere. Yet, all I could think to do in response was scream, "No! I don't want to be strong anymore, I just want to give up!"

Another friend exclaimed in all her wisdom, "God gives suffering to those who possess the strength to endure it." She added, "I am not built like you; I would have lost my sanity if this had happened to me," confirming her mortality but robbing me of mine. I didn't know how to respond to this. How could she be so certain that I wasn't teetering on the brink of madness, that I did indeed have the strength to carry this trauma? Did her statement imply that I somehow deserved this fate because I was stronger? I was left utterly baffled.

I found only alienation and isolation in every corner I looked. I felt terribly lonely and abandoned.

Looking back, I now understand that all those people meant well with their quick fixes and classic platitudes. To be fair, no one really knows the depths of grief unless they have plunged into its bottomless oceans themselves. Even if you have known grief up and close, you can't possibly grasp the overwhelmingly raw emotions of the first few months if you are not yourself in those first few months at the moment. Once those initial months pass, you might still be able to empathise but not as absolutely, not as fiercely.

***

Since I failed to gather validation for my grief from friends and family, I turned elsewhere. I began unloading my uncontainable rage on a social media page that I had created just a few days after Abhinav's death. Surprisingly, my online rants felt immensely liberating. Using the "crazy widow" card that I now had, I voiced my agony without any burden of judgement, and it made me feel empowered in a strange masochistic way.

I could sense the presence of the many who watched me silently as I went on my rampage online; who watched my tragedy unfold and saw me slowly grow deranged. It was as if I was drowning, gasping for air; while everyone else stared at me, nonchalantly, wondering when I would eventually drown and stop making all those noises. Perhaps some of them wanted to help but didn't know how. Perhaps I *wanted* their help but didn't know how to ask for it.

My online outbursts did have a silver lining. They helped me get in touch with several other COVID-19 widows. Scattered all over the country, they were as forlorn as I was, subjected to the same hurtful platitudes by well-meaning family and friends.

We created a WhatsApp group called "Sisters of Grief," a safe space where we could openly talk about aspects of our lives that no one else wanted to hear about—the excruciating pain of the loss of our pasts, futures, physical intimacy and companionship. We exchanged several TED Talk videos, book recommendations and other resources related to grief and loss. We would spontaneously call each other up, cry and listen to stories that seemed so familiar. We didn't have much in common except for the shared pain that had brought us together; their lives were a reflection of my own, echoing the same stories of shattered dreams and futures.

Although our interactions remained confined to the digital realm, engaging with these women brought a sense of relief. I felt seen for the first time in several weeks. All my emotions and reactions felt validated for the very first time.

15

The Otherness of Suffering

Some of what everyone said to pacify me did eventually get to me. I began wondering if I was being way too hysterical, if I was wallowing in way too much unwarranted self-pity. Maybe it wasn't that bad after all, especially when there was constant, soul-crushing suffering unravelling every second in every single corner of the world.

More recently, there were thousands of children who had lost both their parents to the pandemic and were irreversibly robbed of a carefree childhood. There were countless women who had lost the sole breadwinner of their family to COVID-19 and were struggling to make their ends meet and provide for their dependents.

I, in stark contrast, while sitting in my cosy room, with a generous month long paid time off from my employer and with no dependents whatsoever, was going insane about the unfairness of my life. Or perhaps, it was my fairly secure and privileged life that had resulted in my current existential crisis, as it afforded me the time and the comfort to do so.

Despite this realisation, my loss felt humongous.

My agony stemmed from a position of privilege, shaped by my definition of a normal life as an upper middle class dweller in a Tier 1 city in twenty-first century India. The definition that was based on my parochial outlook of the world of my friends, extended family and acquaintances—none of whom were going through what I was.

Perhaps if it was the nineteenth century, where plagues, wars, droughts and famines that would decimate entire communities of the human race were commonplace; where life expectancy was less than thirty years, I would have been more accepting of my situation. I would have been grateful for just being alive.

Perhaps the reason for the moderation of Mom's and Papa's display of grief was that acceptance came a bit easy to them at an age when they had gone through their fair share of tribulations, concluding that "to live means to suffer." They had weathered turbulent times, witnessed the death of their parents, grappled with the losses of close friends and family, and this was yet another blow that had now marred their lives.

While I continued to dwell in my suffering, there were others who came to parade their own in front of me. Some who visited me just after the restrictions were eased, initiated conversations with their own grievances, "I was battling with depression all of last year" or "I am having a hard time adjusting to married life."

I kept quiet and listened, all the while fuming inside.

Did they share their struggles because they pitied me and thought that it would make me feel better knowing that their lives were also somewhat miserable? Was it some form of empathy that I failed to recognize? Or was it a natural reaction to being cooped up in their homes for way too long?

I badly wanted to interrupt their unnecessary monologues—Why are you telling me this? My husband just died, do you really think that I care about your self-induced depression?

Then there were those who began unwittingly competing with me in the "who has suffered more" contest—something I couldn't recall signing up for. They seemed to be determined to prove that their lives were more tragic than mine. I don't know how, but the conversation about my husband's death would often veer off course as they would sigh and remark, "You know, I had a miserable childhood."

This would make my insides boil. I admit it was rather immature of me, but I would often find myself jumping into this implied competition to add something like, "Alright, but do you know that my Mom has been mentally ill since forever???" Boom! I kind of beat you on that one!

I thought, with the multiple untimely deaths in my family and all the ensuing trauma, I had won this contest fair and square. How dare they still have the audacity to compete with me?

I was so engrossed in being a victim of my own pain that I ended up inadvertently diminishing everyone else's. I did that, yes, but then I did something worse. I held my grief above the grief of Abhinav's parents.

While I was infuriated by those comforting me with "at leasts," I used the same "at leasts" on them to assert the superiority of my loss. "At least they have their other son," "At least they have each other," "At least they can share their grief of losing a child with each other, my grief as Abhinav's widow is solitary," "At least they got to live their youth and middle age, I didn't get to live either."

I had become indifferent to the fact that Papa was a father who had just cremated his young son—whom he had nurtured and ensured the best possible upbringing for. My misery made me oblivious to his fears of a looming old age without that son, who was supposed to be a big part of his support system and caregiving.

For Mom, Abhinav was literally an extension of her body, whom she had carried inside her for nine months—birthed him and nourished him to grow into the man who I had eventually come to marry. I was oblivious to her unimaginable pain as well.

I kept rationalising how my angst was more profound than theirs and everyone else's, how life had been more ruthless to me. As if their pain and my pain couldn't coexist. As if there was room for only a limited amount of suffering in the world, and I was greedily trying to grab every bit of it for myself.

My grief, in all its arrogance, had become all-consuming, a raging tyrant that lorded over everyone else's grief.

16

Invoking the Gods

When there is no one in particular to blame, then it is the gods above who must take that blame.

I have never been a religious person. The extent of my religiosity was more or less at par with most people of my generation, where I managed to slip in occasional prayers to the Hindu gods from time to time. I would pray when I thought I was going to fail an exam. I would pray when I desperately wanted to get through a job interview. I would pray during Hindu festivals. I would visit temples on birthdays and death anniversaries.

I was never particularly religious, but deep down, I did believe in the existence of an omnipotent, omnipresent power that called the shots from somewhere up there. For me, it was my hometown's local deity, Bawe Wali Mata, who was the manifestation of that power. However, my faith in her was likely rooted in culture and tradition rather than being driven purely by belief. Some of the most cherished memories from my childhood are trips to her temple located a few kilometres outside the city of Jammu.

On most Sundays, our youngest chacha would stuff the six of us—me, my brother and my four cousins—into our Maruti car and drive us to the mandir. We would stroll down the familiar lane to the temple, flanked on both sides by bustling shops full of beautiful toys, small figurines of Hindu gods and all kinds of stunning imitation jewellery. The halwai shops on the way always smelled tantalisingly of fresh puris and halwa.

Among these shops was Sharma Halwai, where we would make a pit stop to remove our shoes and belts—they were not allowed inside the mandir—and buy some sweet barfi for prasad. We would guard the prasad with our lives as

87

we walked towards the main mandir, terrified that the monkeys along the way would snatch it from us.

At the mandir's entrance, two separate queues would form for men and women. As young children, we would dart from the spot where our chachu stood in line to the front to gauge how quickly we were moving and then run back to inform him of the status. Inching ahead with the queue, I would reach out for the tiny bells suspended above where we stood, swiftly pushing them to make a jingling sound that was immensely melodious to the ears. When I was younger, I had to jump to reach the bells. As I grew taller, I would gleam in secret pride, being able to ring them without a jump.

Once inside the main temple that enshrined the deity, I would try to catch a glimpse of her through the crowd. The moment I caught sight of the idol, I'd close my eyes. With her image still vivid in my mind, I'd quickly make my wish.

We would then merrily make our way back to the halwai shop, dodging the monkeys and enjoying the sweet barfi.

After I relocated from my hometown, every time I returned to see my family, I made it a point to visit the mandir. It had become a homecoming ritual for me. I would pray for my Dad's soul to find peace, for my Mom to forgive her past, and for my brother and me to find more stability in our lives.

When Abhinav came to meet my family for the very first time, I took him to the mandir too. It was only logical.

I'm not particularly religious, but just before my first Diwali as a married woman, I bought my own first-ever mandir. It was a small wooden structure, a miniature replica of the south Indian temples known for their intricate carvings. We decided to pin it to the wall of our study and, inside it, I placed small idols of many gods and goddesses - Ganesh, Lakshmi, Ram, Sita and Hanuman that Abhinav's father, Papa, had gifted me from his own mandir.

I am not a religious person, but when Abhinav was battling for his life in the hospital and it seemed like the doctors were running out of options, as a knee-jerk reaction, I began praying to all the Hindu gods that I could think of. During those long nights spent waiting outside the ICU, I played the Hanuman Chalisa on repeat on my phone and listened to it through my headphones. Pacing up and down a corridor, I would also offer my reverence to the big mighty Ganesh idol that was placed at the end of the entrance. Deeply distressed, I would try to make eye contact with the idol, attempting to get through to the deity to convey how crucial Abhinav's survival was.

I didn't want to waste a second not spend fervently pleading with the gods to spare Abhinav's life, afraid of their wrath if I faltered. I felt convinced that they were scrutinising my every move. One wrong step, one minute not spent devoted to them, could cost Abhinav his life. I feared the gods then like I had never feared them before.

I also frequently remembered my long-gone Dad, something I hadn't done with such intensity in several months. The last time I had thought about him so profoundly was during my wedding, more than a year ago. I wholeheartedly believed that even if the gods may not heed my pleas, but my Dad would; he would definitely come to my rescue. He wouldn't let this happen to me again.

I also found myself scrolling through the dozen or so crowdsourcing NGOs online, raising funds to support the less fortunate grappling with COVID-19. I donated thousands of rupees every day. Each time I saw Abhinav's reports—deteriorating—I donated five thousand rupees. Every time his oxygen levels plummeted further, I sent another five thousand rupees. When he was moved to the ICU, an additional ten thousand rupees went their way. I remained on this giving spree until we finally lost him.

My donations, it seems, were never intended for the needy. They were intended for my own sake. My newfound altruism was perhaps an attempt to barter with God—charity in return for my husband's life. All the last-minute prayers were in desperation to save him. All this charade was in an effort to seek instant redemption; in the hope that some power somewhere would notice my actions and reward me with a last-minute miracle.

Is that why I was not salvaged? Is my sporadic devotion the reason I was punished the way I was?

While I did what I could at the eleventh hour, Mom and Papa, having done this for decades, devoted all their waking hours to their beloved gods. I was certain that at least their pleas to save Abhinav would be effective. They were slowly recovering from COVID-19 themselves, but would sit still in the pooja room for hours at a stretch- like tapasvis beseeching their gods and asking them for forgiveness.

If I were indeed punished for my last minute reverence, why were Mom and Papa penalised? Shouldn't God have favoured them for their years of devotion, thousands of hours of prayers and the hundreds of temples they have visited in their lifetime? Isn't that how religion is supposed to work?

Or did my nonchalance towards religion outweigh their faith in this particular case? Was God really that vengeful?

When tragedy finally struck, it made me question whatever limited faith I had in God. Every night in the weeks following Abhinav's passing, I found myself sitting on the balcony of Mom and Papa's home in the middle of the night for hours on end. Gazing up into the dark expanse, I would demand answers. I would scream into the clear June nights, "What are you trying to teach me now? Have I not learned enough! What had Abhinav ever done to deserve it? Tell me why? Come down right away and tell me why!"

***

The gods were not going to come down to parley with a lunatic woman; I had to take my questions elsewhere. So I turned to Papa.

For as long as I have known him, Papa has been reasonably devout. Ever since his retirement, I had witnessed him adhering to the same daily routine with unwavering commitment: after returning from his morning walk, he would don his white lungi and vest, wear a rudraksha mala around his neck and decorate his forehead with saffron tilak. He would retreat to the pooja room for hours at end, only taking breaks for his meals. Every now and then, much like a proud young child showing off his toys, he would give me an enthusiastic tour of his mandir and showcase his treasured collection of idols.

Given his deep knowledge and experience on the subject, I turned to Papa. My quest wasn't solely driven by helplessness, sorrow or anger; I genuinely believed that somewhere within the vast corpus of Hindu scriptures out there—the Gita, the Upanishads, the Mahabharata and others—there should be words of wisdom that answer my questions; if not, at the very least, soothe my troubled mind.

At the time, Papa was too melancholic himself to indulge my questions. Nonetheless, he humoured me and said, "Perhaps it is the karmic balance that we carry on from our past lives. Perhaps we were sinful men and women in our previous incarnations and are now paying the price for those sins."

I nodded in agreement, but I was far from satisfied with that answer.

I have never really believed in karmic balance spanning multiple lifetimes. Karma, for one, had always been an abstract bogeyman to me, devised by our ancestors to trick future generations into behaving, preventing them from unleashing the full potential of human monstrosity.

It also appeared that the concept of karma might have stemmed from the human brain's desire to impose rationality to everything that happens. Everything must follow a logic; everything must have an explanation. We feel less in control when we are unable to attach reasoning to an event. There had to be a reason for "why Abhinav," for "why me." It couldn't all just be arbitrary; it couldn't all just be random. Life is just the coming together of a gazillion random events is unimaginable to us. It is unacceptable to us that there is no such thing as karma, that there is perhaps no such thing as God.

***

I remember closely observing the rituals that we performed in the wake of Abhinav's passing. The cremation and the scattering of the ashes in the holy Ganga was followed by everyday poojas. A priest came to the house to preside over those and Papa partook in them sincerely. Then there were other customs; we refrained from consuming certain foods for thirteen days, and during the period, we were supposed to feed stray animals, a supposed conduit to Abhinav, making sure he was receiving that nourishment.

Abhinav's family had fewer customs that they observed after death than mine. I recollected how there was a much more exhausting list of things to do when my dad had died. My brother had to shave his head and sleep on the floor for a few weeks. We had to organise a large feast to feed a hundred mourners who had arrived to grieve on Dad's tenth day of passing.

I wondered why the customs had to punish the grieving this way when they were already tormented by their loss.

Or maybe those are not meant to be punishments. Maybe the purpose of those customs was something else. Maybe it was to help find closure—

something akin to a ScoopWhoop article, "Ten Things to Do to Get Over Your Dead Loved One." It was almost as if we were being reassured by the customs—if you follow these ten rules and conduct these five poojas, your loved one will be taken care of by us; you wouldn't have to worry about them anymore. You can go back to living your lives as you were, unbothered by your loss.

But once the poojas are over, the pandits have left with the leftover pooja flowers and incense sticks and the grieving guests have returned to their lives, the customs and the religion don't tell you what to do with the unrelenting pain that still lingers. It's as though they assume that there should be no pain left. They don't come to your rescue anymore.

After the rituals concluded, Papa kept his pooja room locked for several days. Perhaps he, too, was angry with his gods for their betrayal. It was understandable. However, a few weeks later, I caught him unlocking the room and washing his pooja utensils in preparation for daily prayers.

It triggered me immediately. Furious, I confronted him then and there, "How could you still have faith when your gods failed you in the most trying of times! What else would shake your faith if not this? How could you still believe that there is a God!"

On the verge of tears, he responded, "But this is the only way I know how to live."

Ashamed of my outburst, I stormed out of the pooja room. I realised how diabolical my confrontation was. I had tried to take away the one thing that gave him solace, simply because there was nothing—no faith, no God, no religion, no spirituality—that gave *me* solace as I writhed in pain. His was an unwavering, undeniable faith, the one you never question, but also the one that rewards you by holding you together in trying times. A faith that was entirely alien to me.

Maybe God does not exist, but maybe faith in some sort of higher power is what has kept generations of mankind from an absolute collapse in the face of suffering. People who believe in God, who have faith in a force bigger than them, may be delusional, but maybe we all need some sort of delusion to persevere through times that seem hopeless.

Some of my "Sisters in Grief" also turned to God and spiritual gurus in search of answers to the "whys." Videos circulated in our WhatsApp group titled, "Why do some people die early?" and "What happens to the spirits of our loved ones?" In one such video, a godwoman proclaimed with certainty, "The spirits of your deceased loved ones are still close to you."

Although I desperately wanted Abhinav to be around me, all this spiritual mumbo jumbo didn't resonate with me; neither did it provide any respite. One thing was clear as day to me: Abhinav was nowhere around me; he had been reduced to ashes that were collected in an urn and scattered in a river. And from that moment on, he had ceased to exist all together.

One particular video, in which a Hindu godman was explaining death and grief, triggered me immensely. It lingered on my mind for several days. In it, the spiritual leader was sitting on a stage inside a large auditorium. A disciple from the audience took the mic to ask, "How does one cope with the pain of losing a loved one?"

The godman smirked and began to explain, "We are all just tiny blips on this planet. People are being born, people are dying every day, every minute, every second. So what is the point of fretting over it? Our little lives are inconsequential in the grand scheme of things." The auditorium erupted in thunderous applause.

I was baffled at this line of thought, at how openly it was being welcomed. What the godman had said was the practical, harsh truth about life and death, yes; but the statement felt completely devoid of all human compassion. I wondered if the godman had ever experienced the unexpected death of a loved one. Had he ever cradled the head of his wife, his daughter, his son close to his body as they breathed their last? And if he had, were those his very sentiments at the time— that they were inconsequential blips whose passing didn't warrant any grief.

I couldn't bear to think of Abhinav as a tiny blip, and if he were, then my grief and pain were perhaps even more inconsequential blips. And I couldn't accept that either.

Everyone around me—Abhinav's parents, my "Sisters in Grief," my cousins who were grieving my buji's death clung tightly to their faith in their moments of uncertainty and hopelessness. And I couldn't fathom why.

Why, after all this treachery, did they continue to believe? What fuelled their belief in the benevolence of their gods now? Was it faith, or was it surrender masked as faith, stemming from a fear of offending the gods who, like unruly dictators, might take away whatever little was left of us?

I, on the other hand, was adamant on rejecting this tyranny of the gods. I removed whatever little existence of religion I had in my life. I relinquished the temple that I had so eagerly bought a few months ago and returned the idols to Papa. They no longer served any purpose in my home. I didn't visit Bawe Wali Mata after Abhinav's death because I believed there was nothing she could do for me now. I was prepared to hold this grudge against the gods until they accepted the blame I lay upon them, until my very last breath.

Part IV

Living Without Him: My Father

17

The Amnesia of Childhood

There is not much I remember of my childhood. While I can recall the general themes of the time, I am unable to remember a lot about specific events.

I remember my father being an emotionally distant and stern man whom I feared greatly in my early years; and years later, he morphed into a middle-aged man drowning in despair as he grappled with his deteriorating health.

I remember my mother being a perpetually silent woman who grew even quieter with time. Her silences would often be punctuated with isolated incidents of psychotic outbursts later in life.

I remember them having a strained relationship.

I grew up in our ancestral home in Jammu, which, along with my parents and brother, also housed: my father's two younger brothers and one sister (my buji), their spouses and children. Having half a dozen kids of roughly the same age under one roof was a much-needed respite for all the children, from the tension and drama of the adults.

There are some fleeting snippets that I do remember: forming teams to play hide-and-seek, having rollerblade skating competitions, eagerly tuning in to watch Bournvita Quiz Contest every Sunday morning and attempting to guess the correct answers before the contestants did.

I remember us watching Cartoon Network every evening at five in the living room, keeping a vigilant eye on the front gate of our house, the hurried scramble to our respective rooms to grab our books at the sound of my bade chacha's scooter that signalled his and my Dad's return from work.

I also remember how every summer chote chachu would create a makeshift swimming pool for us by filling the sloped, cemented area at the back of our house with water. I spent countless summer afternoons splashing with my cousins in that pool, laughing and enjoying the cool sweetness of watermelon slices.

In the present day, whenever we get together during festivals or when I am visiting home, my cousins often talk about a few other specific memories: a trip we took together, a relative whose gestures we used to mimic, a stray dog we adopted for a couple of days before we were asked to give it away.

Sadly, I struggle to recall these events that they remember so vividly. While they laugh heartily, I reach into the depths of my psyche trying to locate those memories, but they remain elusive. I nod and chuckle in agreement, pretending. I steal a glance at my brother, trying to gauge if he is faking it too. I am unable to tell.

There is a sense of persistent amnesia about the past that I try to camouflage. Perhaps I was never present as a child, just as I am never present as an adult. My absent-mindedness is perhaps not that recent.

Still, I trust my cousins with their recollections, and this time around, I try to be attentive. I try to take comprehensive mental notes to store these events securely in the vault of my memories. I wouldn't want to be caught unawares the next time.

These occasional catch-ups with my extended family are comforting. They are reminders of the good times of the past. They are reminders of the fact that I was not entirely stripped of the joys of growing up, a notion I, perhaps frivolously, entertain sometimes. All these memories reassure me that my childhood was maybe not as troubled as I sometimes make it out to be in my head. Perhaps I unnecessarily exaggerate.

Or it could be that that's how most children grew up in the nineties. It is true that the nineties were not the time when middle-class families engaged in conversations about feelings and emotions, or trauma and abuse. Everyday conflicts were a common occurrence in most households, especially if large extended families lived under one roof. Children were merely mouths to be fed, their school fees paid in the hope that at least one of them would grow up to become a doctor and be the pride of the family.

I did have my own reasons to doubt my family's normalcy. I knew from a very early age that there was something amiss, something dysfunctional, something anxiety-inducing about my home—a feeling notably absent from my nani's house.

Summer vacations were undeniably the highlight of the year. We would pack our bags, grab a bunch of Champak comics and hop on a bus headed for Nani's house. It was a house that echoed with ceaseless laughter and animated conversations, where children were not merely ignored until mealtimes but often involved in all activities by the adults.

My mamus would engage in flirtatious banter with their wives, often joke with Nani, and even play all kinds of board games with their children. My cousins at Nani's home were free to jump around the house with carefree abandon, and their fluffy white Pomeranian, Rosie, sprang alongside them with equal excitement.

All of this was in stark contrast to everything I saw back home.

As a child, I was amazed by the joy that I felt in Nani's house and, as an adult, I desperately sought that comfort everywhere. I cherished those fifteen-odd days when I could pretend to belong to this harmonious family, before reluctantly packing my bags to return to my own—a family marked by notable discontent and conflict.

18

My Father who Loved Me

In appearance, my father bore a striking resemblance to the quintessential father figure often depicted in 90s Bollywood movies, mainly there for comic relief—the happy-go-lucky middle-aged man with a stumpy stature and a protruding belly, who could frequently be seen donning a brimmed beret, cracking unoriginal dad jokes for the pleasure of all and sundry.

In temperament, however, he was the opposite. There were no dad jokes at all; instead, his demeanour was marked with big bloodshot eyes and a thunderous voice that could send shivers down one's spine.

He had a difficult start to his life. Having lost both his parents by the time he turned twenty, the burden of sustaining the family financially fell upon him and his younger siblings. That did explain some of his stiffness and the inherent moroseness of my chachas.

I was, undeniably, terrified of my father, but I was also proud of him. He was a scientist at a local research laboratory affiliated to the Council of Scientific & Industrial Research. I loved bragging about him to my friends. Their curiosity about him being a *'scientist'* would often solicit questions like, "Has he ever been to space?" I would explain, beaming with pride, "No, but he is involved in a very big research project on cancer right now and has so many expensive machines in his office!" If some of them weren't impressed by that, I'd add, "He also has a bunch of adorable guinea pigs in his lab. I can take you there sometime."

He was, in fact, the first person in our family to travel abroad for work, a significant feat for any one of us at the time. It happened when I was around 10 years old and he got the opportunity to spend two months working on a research project in Germany. I vividly recall the day he returned. Our entire extended family, more than a dozen people, gathered at the Jammu railway station to welcome him back with marigold garlands. I saw tears trickle down his weathered face for the very first time.

Despite having extensively travelled internationally, my Dad's heart was rooted deep in Jammu. He received several enticing job offers from prestigious research laboratories in Delhi and Germany, but he turned them all down. He couldn't fathom the idea of leaving Jammu and his father's house behind; even as over the years, the same house became a source of unrelenting anxiety for him and everyone else.

Living under the same roof for several decades, conflict had started emerging among the siblings, as is often the case in joint families. These conflicts became more pronounced as we, the children, grew older. However, despite the growing tensions, there was never a question of moving out of the ancestral house for any of the four families.

That unsaid, unwavering attachment to the house originally stemmed, I believe, from the fact that my deceased grandfather had laid down the very foundation of it. The four siblings had gradually built it up from there, brick by brick, room by room, as their own families grew in size.

Soon, I began to think of the house as a chamber of endless pandemonium, and I failed to understand why we couldn't just leave. Why couldn't the brothers just sit together and talk it out? Why couldn't Dad just accept one of those job offers away from here?

Regrettably, none of that happened. Instead, over time, the inanimate structure of the house became paramount, even over the combined sanity of the sixteen people inhabiting it.

What also surprised me was that despite all its alleged significance, the house never saw any renovations. As a result, the structure continued to fall apart over the years. The paint adorning the living room was horribly chipped, ancient furniture occupied every corner, strained curtains gathered dust as nobody bothered to change them and the fragile boundary walls were on the verge of collapsing. It was as if the broken relationships, the resentment and the paranoia that reigned over our minds were all manifesting into the brokenness of the house.

***

Given his strictness and ill-temper, I kept my distance from my father, which is why I knew only a few things about him; but among those few things, I was absolutely certain of only one—that my father loved me.

At the risk of sounding cocky, I do have to give myself some credit for that. I was the child who met the most expectations of a promising offspring in a typical middle-class household. I consistently earned decent grades at school, steered clear of trouble and displayed blind obedience to my father. Of course, this obedience didn't necessarily come to me naturally; a great part of it stemmed from my desire to earn his approval, while the remaining was the result of a deeply ingrained fear of him.

My brother, on the other hand, was the complete opposite and would often find his own ways to rebel against my father. Much to my father's continued disappointment, he showed very little inclination towards academics, faced occasional suspensions from school and was audacious enough to pursue his interest in football. He would often be punished for his digressions in the form of my father's thrashing, which, as he grew older, didn't seem to bother or hurt him anymore.

By all conventional standards, I shined in comparison.

My father loved me, but he could never articulate that love in clear, crisp language—most fathers of that generation are perhaps notoriously stingy with expressions of their affection. However, he did manage to show some of that love in his own strange ways.

For instance, I would find him announcing with pride, "My daughter got through all the colleges whose exams she sat for; she even got through the government colleges." In those rare moments, I would stand by his side, modesty personified, my hands clasped behind me, while a flush of glory and joy brushed through my soul.

I know my father loved me, but I often wonder if his love for me was truly unconditional, like the love of a parent is supposed to be. I wonder sometimes, had I not been the obedient and academically competent child that I was and, instead, had turned out to be another *'disappointment'* to him—like he thought my mother and my brother were—would he still have loved me the same way? Would he still have praised me, still talked about me with the same spark in his eyes? Or was I merely a medium to elevate his own self-worth?

It is a question that would, unfortunately, remain unanswered.

I know my father loved me, but over time, I grew to resent him deeply. I couldn't bring myself to reciprocate whatever little affection he managed to shower upon me. My resentment towards him was not because of who he was to me but rather because of who he was to my mother.

I despised that he wasn't capable of having a reasonable conversation with her, that he wouldn't use her name when talking about her or *to* her, instead, just shout out vague pronouns, as if she was not human, as if they were not closely related. I despised that he was tirelessly vexed and disgruntled with her for things that were too trivial to justify his displeasure.

I know my father loved me, but I couldn't love him back because I couldn't disentangle the father he was to me from the husband he was to my mother.

19

My Mother who Couldn't

My mother was vastly different from the other women I had known growing up—my buji, my chachis, my nani, my mamis. She was, in fact, the most reclusive woman I had ever known.

During weddings and family gatherings, while the other women in the family could be found engaging in gossip with carefree abandon, my mother, who appeared to be in great discomfort, would politely greet everyone and retreat to a quiet corner, her hands clasped tightly around her chest, as if keeping her heart together by sheer force. Nodding as if she was listening, but in reality, every fibre of her being wanted to escape, not just from that moment but from her entire life. Anyone who observed her could discern that she didn't quite fit in, and, more importantly, that she had no desire to.

I don't recall my mother being an involved parent either; she has always been largely disinterested in the details of my life. Whether I was getting proper nutrition, which school I went to, which college I attended, which city I was currently residing in—she had, and still maintains, absolutely no awareness of these or other aspects of my life. This was in stark contrast to my chachis, who would eagerly rush to enquire about my cousins' day as soon as they returned from school.

At first, I assumed that her neglect was only reserved for me and that she adored my brother. But as I grew up, I realised that she was equally dismissive of him. It is only now that I understand that her disdain wasn't driven by an inherent dislike for us, but was a manifestation of her trauma that she continued to endure alone, that fuelled her aversion to everything that was associated with it, including the children that she had birthed.

In the early years of her marriage, my father's ill temper was met with silence from her. But as time passed, her response evolved into hysterical outbursts, attempting to match his aggression with an equal, or sometimes even louder, screaming. My once-timid mother underwent a dramatic transformation with time, becoming a maniac, ready to launch into a rage-fuelled rant at the slightest provocation.

The hysteria that she embodied to counter my father never truly left her body. It continues to live in her even today, nearly a decade after his death, like a tool pertinent to her survival.

One moment, she is sitting in absolute silence, lost in her own world. The next, she has burst into a torrent of psychotic explosion. "You don't know what happened to me!" "Nobody was there by my side!" "Nobody supported me!" "I was alone and I still am!" She goes on with this monologue for thirty minutes or so, until her throat grows parched.

I never fully understood what was behind those outbursts. While I had hoped that time would gradually heal her and things would eventually improve, the trauma she carries is so deeply ingrained that it has become a permanent and integral part of her identity.

Though her rants are seldom coherent, she is undeniably right about one thing: she *was* all alone through the worst of it.

In her outbursts, she often recounts how she had sought refuge with Nanu-Nani when she first met with my father's rage in the early years of her marriage, when I was just a toddler. But they insisted that she return to him and reconcile with him. She kept going to them for help over and over again, but they kept sending her back. Until she gave up and didn't return anymore.

Not only her parents, but her very own daughter—me—had betrayed her.

I remember that fateful night vividly. I was in my room after dinner, busy with my studies for my class 10th Board exams, when I heard a heated argument erupt in my parents' room. It was a familiar occurrence of every other night, so I did not pay much attention to it initially.

I could hear both of them screeching at the top of their voices, so I tried to block my ears with my fingers to avoid the distraction. The next thing I knew, thudding sounds began to emanate from their room. Alarmed, I dashed to check what had happened. The door was partially bolted so I flung it open. I found both of them standing, pausing from whatever they were up to as they turned to look at me.

My mother was positioned close to the door, whimpering, and my father stood a few feet away from her, huffing with fury. A stream of blood gushed out of the ridge of my mother's nose.

Seeing my mother with a broken nose, a surge of anger coursed through me. I wanted to hit my father with all the strength that I could muster and break his nose as well. In fact, I wanted to kill him right there for what he had done to her.

I looked at him, all rage.

However, as I locked my eyes with the man standing before me, who, despite being just over five feet four inches tall, was still formidable, his bloodshot eyes frightened me to my core. I stood there, frozen, for what seemed like an eternity. I did absolutely nothing at all.

As my mother hurried to the washroom, I tried to walk my immobile body back to my room. Even though she walked around with a huge visible scar on her nose for the next several days, nobody questioned her or my father about what had transpired.

A deluge of guilt sinks my heart whenever I am reminded of that incident. I failed to protect my mother; I didn't stand up for her when she needed me the most.

As I have replayed that incident hundreds of times in my mind over the last several years, I have contemplated the alternative actions that I could have taken that day, had I not been the coward that I was. I could have grabbed the landline phone that sat next to the bed and struck my father with it, I could have simply screamed at him and called him out for the despicability.

Instead, I had stood there frozen, like a fool.

It torments me every day to think that if only I had done something that day, perhaps my mother wouldn't have felt that alone, that abandoned all her life. Perhaps she wouldn't have grown so distanced from me, and perhaps I would have had the mother that I always longed for.

Considering how I failed her, her indifference toward me feels completely justified. I, her child, had deserted her when she needed me the most. I understood her detachment and that she owed me nothing. The rational part of my brain understood all of that, but my vulnerable heart couldn't come to accept it; it continued to crave her affection and attention all my life.

When Abhinav passed, I expected my mother to come running to me, to pull me into her embrace. I wanted her to hold me, to assure me that she was going to help me get through this pain. I wanted her to say that she would be there by my side. I wanted her to sit with me and listen to me while I whined endlessly for hours about how terribly it hurt.

But when she didn't even bother to call me even once, I was consumed by an anger so primal, I saw red. This thing that had happened to me was enormous; it was life-shattering. She had to care; how could she not care? I am her child!

I often think about how I have forgiven my father, while I continue to resent my mother. I forgave him for not being the father I wanted him to be, but for some reason, I am unable to forgive my mother. Could it be that death has erased the expectations that I had set for him? But I continue to burden her with those same expectations, unfairly, her only fault being that she continues to live.

20

The Trauma That Spilled Over

Our parents are our first heroes, the first humans we look up to and try to emulate. Yet, as we grow older, there comes a day when we realise that they, too, are flawed, riddled with insecurities and shortcomings, not as perfect as we had once perceived them to be. We lose a little bit of our heroes that day.

However, there is also a part of that ideal that stays intact in perpetuity. It could be something about their value system that we continue to hold in high regard, or it is their extraordinary patience in dealing with, say, the sluggish processes of government offices that we admire. In one way or another, there is always a piece of that hero, who is now slowly beginning to look a little feeble, that still manages to shine come what may.

For me and my brother, both our heroes fell quite early on—and they fell hard.

From a relatively early age, I could tell that they were indeed flawed. But, it is only now that I have come to accept that their flaws were not inherent, rather, they were a result of their circumstances, their own unique traumas. The real tragedy, however, lies in the fact that that trauma was so intense and so permeable that it couldn't possibly remain contained within their bodies. It spilled over and flooded the lives of both their children as well.

As their altercations would transpire in the room that was separated from the bedroom that my brother and I shared by just a small living room, we would continue with our everyday lives, largely unfazed. We had grown to accept the daily commotion as a part of our existence. We would talk and laugh about the mundane things, bicker like siblings are supposed to, fight over trivialities like cupboard space, draw boundary lines in the room and borrow each other's belongings.

But sometimes the tension in the other room would build up beyond the usual. When that would happen, we would suffer in isolation and in absolute silence. As the decibels of the sound emanating from that wretched room would rise, my heart would sink with anxiety.

I couldn't tell if my brother's heart sank the same, he would never speak to me about it, just as I never broached the subject with him. Our parents, in addition to isolating themselves from us, had also succeeded in isolating us from each other, ruthlessly stripping us off all possible emotional dimensionality.

The day Abhinav passed away, my brother was the first person I called; he was in Jammu at the time. As I sobbed uncontrollably, he wept on the other end of the line, speaking words that I was unable to decipher. But his choked voice resurrected the memories of the last time we had cried together like this. The time when we weren't separated by hundreds of kilometres, like we were now, and were instead sitting side by side in a hospital in Jammu. My brother had just returned from his college in Punjab, before Dad drew his last breaths a couple of hours later.

Only nineteen at the time, he had sat beside me, with tears streaming down his face. In all his innocence, he had asked, "Did he know that I was here, that I had come back for him? Was he in his senses enough to know that?"

Dad wasn't. He had been unconscious for the past few days. But I couldn't rob my brother of his only remaining solace. So I had lied and reassured him, "He was. He knew you were here."

***

Following Abhinav's passing, my brother insisted on coming to visit me, but I adamantly refused. I didn't see any point in it. He did, however, faithfully continue to call me every day. Not really knowing what to say, he would simply ask me each time, "How are you?" And I would respond with a plain, "I am doing okay," when in reality, I wanted to burst out into so much more.

Tragically, neither of us possessed the courage to talk about emotions and feelings and loss and misery. Even in the midst of such a heart-wrenching tragedy and such insurmountable pain, we remained incapable of summoning courage. Courage to finally cross the bridge of emotional distance that our parents had built with their own distance, that stood strong between the two of us, mocking us cruelly.

How I wish I could talk to him! How I wish I could cry to him!

Because he, of all people, understood the true depth of my loss. He was the one who really knew the history of my suffering, for it was his history of suffering as well.

The unsaid bond that they say that siblings share, irrespective of how their lives branch out with time, is not because of the shared blood that runs into their veins, but because of the shared history that moulds their lives and the shared trauma that mars it.

21

Escaping My Reality

By the time I was in my late teens, I was convinced that the only way I could save myself was by escaping from my home in Jammu and my family. So when a Mumbai-based IT company came to recruit from my college, I jumped at the opportunity.

My father wasn't too pleased with my decision. He voiced multiple concerns, "They are offering you such a meagre salary; you could earn the same amount in Jammu and save much more." "The cost of living in Mumbai is exorbitant." "It is not safe for girls in big cities." But my mind was already made up. I had to leave to protect my own sanity.

Mumbai amazed me in so many ways. At first, the fast lives, the traffic, the local trains, the towering buildings were all very overwhelming and a stark contrast from the slow life I lived in Jammu. But soon, I began to embrace it all, with arms wide open, as my new home.

I shared a two-bedroom apartment on the eighth floor of a ten-story high-rise building with three other women. The living room of the flat boasted a huge floor-to-ceiling window that offered a view of the balconies in front of us and the several little stories unfolding in each of them—a newlywed couple enjoying their tea sitting on collapsible chairs, a middle-aged man giving a bath to his adorable little beagle pup, an elderly woman oiling a young girl's luscious hair.

My building and a few others stood surrounding a large park where most evenings, children could be found on the swings while their mothers gathered on the benches in groups of twos and threes, engaged in lively conversations. People watching, especially after returning from the office, became my favourite form of unwinding.

Even the Mumbai rains lived up to the hype. Whenever it rained, our cook, a lovely middle-aged Maharashtrian lady, would whip up crisp bhajiya and adrak chai for us. Lounging on the mattresses in our living room, we would relish those snacks, silently savouring the tipper-tapper melody of the rain for hours together.

There were no arguments, no shouting, no sudden noises to trigger my anxiety. I felt the kind of uninterrupted sweet lull that had eluded me my whole life. I breathed a sigh of relief, claiming my freedom from my other life that continued to play at the same rhythm as I had left it, only now without me.

Luckily, I shared a decent relationship with my flatmates. The four of us would huddle together in the living room for hours at night—sometimes we'd watch movies, and other times we'd simply giggle the night away discussing boys, fashion and everything else under the sun.

On most Friday nights, we'd board the local train to Marine Drive, where we'd sit on the concrete track by the shore and whisper into each other's ears, our dreams, aspirations and hopes for the future. The sound of the waves crashing against the rocks was always therapeutic, as if those waves were washing away all that had built up over the past few years—the anxieties, the regrets—making way for the new and the unknown that held promise.

I would close my eyes, inhaling the cool crisp breeze wafting off the waves, and silently promise myself, "This new life, so sacred and pristine—I will never let my past muddle it."

By then, my brother had also moved to another city to study engineering. Although we were physically apart, I was comforted by the knowledge that we were both safe, far from the place we once called home.

The only souvenirs here, from my life back home, were the daily phone calls from my Dad, which served as reminders of the fact that I was free, yet so tied to my past.

I dreaded those calls, which would follow more or less the same script for fifteen-odd minutes—the first five minutes, he would plead with me to return home; for the remaining ten, he would launch into a series of tirades about his deteriorating relationships with my chachus, my mother's escalating violence and his bewilderment at my choice to move to a place where I slept on a mattress on the floor.

The distress in his voice was palpable. Yet, by that time, my resentment towards him had grown by leaps and bounds. I responded to his long rants with monosyllables.

I never heard from my mother.

It wasn't until I began working in Mumbai that I discovered my father was severely diabetic, and he had been keeping it a secret from all of us for quite some time. I stumbled upon some prescription medications for diabetes in his drawer during a visit home. It didn't startle me as much; both my chachas had been successfully managing diabetes for more than a decade by then and had it under control with medication and insulin injections. I assumed that my father would manage much the same.

I couldn't have been more wrong. Over the course of the next two years, the illness plagued and devoured his body at such an alarming pace that it left everyone horrified and bewildered. Within that short span, he went from being merely a diabetic to losing the majority of his eyesight in both eyes and suffering significant decline in his kidney function. All of it happened so quickly that it allowed us very little time to understand and react to it. It was all the more perplexing because the same disease, the same progression had taken around ten to fifteen years in my chachas.

My father would return from the office, change into his vest and pyjamas and sit in one corner of his bed, lost in rumination for hours on end. Often, he would break down in front of us and others. He was convinced that the disease would destroy him, that everything he had built so far would be taken away, and that we, his children, were headed for doom without him.

I couldn't bring myself to look at him as he drowned himself in this ocean of despair. I couldn't believe that my once intimidating father had transformed into this ball of self-pity and hopelessness, and his once commanding voice had given way to anxious, timid sobs.

He lost upwards of twenty kilos in just over two years; one could see loose skin hanging from his forearms when he would wear his sleeveless vests. The muscles in his face had vanished to reveal the skeletal structure underneath. Small wounds dotted his entire upper body and never seemed to heal, even with all the talcum and gels he would apply to soothe them. His once protruding belly was no longer protruding; he had to wear his belts several notches in to fit his now oversized pants.

I often wonder if this rapid progression of the disease was indeed natural and if it was really his body that was giving up, or was it, in fact, the doings of his mind that accelerated the deterioration?

Was it the loneliness he felt in the house that was thronging with people? Was it the anxiety about his children and their future? Was it his disappointment in his wife? Was it his paranoia about his brothers and the ongoing family disputes? Or was it a concoction of all of it put together?

Regardless of what the reasons were, his relentless worrying continued to demolish him from the inside.

How I wish I could travel back in time and give him a glimpse of the future, at least of the time just before Abhinav's death—to show him that everything turned out fine, that the unrelenting worry that killed him was unwarranted. That I managed to establish a decent living for myself, that I no longer slept on mattresses on the floor, that I did end up meeting a wonderful man to marry, that my brother did end up securing a decent job.

How I wish I could show him the content, confident faces of his children from the future, dispelling all his unfounded fears. It was only this glimpse of the future, and nothing else, that could have saved him back then.

22

Not Getting Any Better

The year leading up to my father's death was the most daunting for him; to say he was miserable would be an understatement.

By that time, he had lost nearly all sight in both his eyes. With over 60% of his kidneys declared damaged, he was compelled to start on daily hemodialysis, initially once a day and soon advancing to twice a day.

A fine incision was made in his abdomen to insert a catheter that was then attached to his kidneys. The exposed part of the catheter would permanently hang from his body, which when not in use, he would secure to his stomach with tape. To perform the dialysis procedure, we had engaged a nurse who would visit our home twice daily. Before commencing each session, he would meticulously sterilise my parents' bedroom to prevent any chance of infection, which could prove deadly for my father.

Throughout the whole procedure, two plastic bags would be attached to that catheter through additional tubes. One bag, containing a fresh solution that was supposed to circulate through my father's body, would hang from a stand overhead. Simultaneously, the second bag would be placed on the floor to collect the toxins drained out of his body. The two bags together were essentially performing the function of his failing kidneys.

As the cold fluid coursed through his frail body, my father would shiver incessantly. Unable to cope with the physical discomfort of it all and consumed by an unrelenting anxiety about what the future held, he would spend the remainder of the day in tears. When his throat grew parched from the sobbing, he would ask for water, but he had to be denied. The doctors had instructed us to restrict his water intake to avoid any further strain on his already distressed kidneys. Disheartened, he would proceed to sob some more.

It was an endless cycle of agony, for him and for us.

I couldn't bear to witness my father's suffering any longer; something had to be done immediately. I decided to reach out to a few doctors in a prestigious hospital in Delhi to seek their guidance. After sharing his medical reports via email and engaging in a few follow-up discussions, what became evident was that we could get his eyes operated on, and then eventually work towards securing a kidney for transplant.

This revelation was like a silver lining, sparking hope in me—once he regains his sight, he might be able to return to work. That would give his days routine and, possibly, revive some of his motivation. It will also buy us time to contemplate the next steps.

With this plan in mind, I took an extended leave from the office and headed to Jammu. I learned to perform dialysis with the guidance of the nurse. I familiarised myself with the sterilisation process, the process of attaching the dialysis bags to the catheter and the proper disposal of the collected fluids. Packing all necessary equipment into my trolley bag, I booked flight tickets for us to Delhi. I was optimistic—we were going to get this resolved.

As I prepared for our departure, I asked my mother to accompany us, thinking it would be good to have another helping hand.

To my utter disbelief, she refused outright.

It was only then that I, for the first time, fully realised the magnitude of the trauma that my father had caused her and the strength of the roots of hatred that he had planted in her. It stunned me.

I knew that she resented Dad, and rightfully so, but I didn't know how much that resentment had grown in the last decade. I didn't realise that she resented him to the point that she wouldn't budge an inch for him; the man who was her husband, the man who was likely dying. I pleaded with her repeatedly, but she was adamant.

So we left without her, just the two of us.

Lying in the ward of the Delhi hospital, a strange transformation occurred in my father. I saw him get hopeful again. He ceased his unrelenting wailing and complaining. Instead, he started talking more about his life, incidents from his childhood and youth, his dreams and aspirations. Sitting beside him in the visitor's bench, I would listen to him, rapt with attention, for hours.

He started to confide in me, "Once I can see again, I promise I will stop worrying. Maybe I can live with the dialysis, as many other people do. Maybe I will take voluntary retirement from work and just tend to our garden. I really want to plant new rose bushes and bougainvillaea. Our mali doesn't do a very good job of it."

Because his vision had deteriorated a lot by that time, I would gently brush his upper arm to signal to him, "Yes, that would be wonderful."

This was the first time that I was encountering this new side to my father—not the strict disciplinarian whom I feared, nor the distressed patient whom I had started to pity. This was someone else, someone harbouring his own independent dreams. Dreams that didn't rely on the reassurance of the stable future of his children, the compliance of his wife, or harmony with his siblings. Dreams that had been suppressed all this while, burdened by the weight of decades of anger, fear and expectations of others; dreams that had suddenly grown wings at the sight of hope again.

It was simply his own dreams for his very own life.

Maybe that is how uncomplicated the essence of all human desire is. Under the mountain of the ever-burgeoning ambitions of hefty salary packages, big flashy cars, travel to exotic locations, quests for perfect soulmates— maybe the real human longing is, after all, *that basic, that unassuming.*

Witnessing him wither in front of my eyes had melted away some of the years of hatred that had built-up inside of me, and it was the first time I had acknowledged how punishing life had been for him. How he had never truly lived for himself. How all his youth had been devoted to stabilising a family shattered by the premature loss of parents, and now, in middle age, he was grappling with a prolonged chronic illness. How exhausting all of it must have been for him.

Perhaps he wasn't the monster I had made him out to be; perhaps all my disgruntlement towards him was unwarranted; perhaps nothing is ever as black and white as we deem it to be; perhaps there were shades of grey that had escaped me.

***

We stayed in that Delhi hospital for about two weeks. A few days in, the doctors attempted to operate on my father's eyes, but because of the precarious condition of the rest of his organs, his vitals began to destabilise and he had to be transferred to the ICU. My brother had joined me by this time.

I distinctly remember both of us sitting outside the ICU in the dead of night, uncertainty and fear looming above us. The waiting room then, was nothing like the turbulent waiting room I had faced when I had waited for Abhinav. It was vast and empty, with very few people, most of whom were hospital staff. It felt eerily quiet.

The doctor-in-charge emerged from the ICU. "Is there someone else, an adult, I can speak to?" he asked, shifting his gaze from me to my brother and then back.

I was twenty-five at the time, but perhaps appeared much younger to him. I rose to my feet and stepped forward. "No, it is just us." The doctor went on, "His vitals fluctuated significantly during our attempt to perform the surgery. Right now, our priority is to stabilise his overall health. Operating the eyes is completely out of the question for now." I nodded. He paused, waiting for me to ask further questions, but I didn't have any.

To our relief, the doctors did manage to stabilise Dad over the next three days. However, they discharged him soon after, since there wasn't much that could be done given his condition. Taking Dad back was an even more arduous task. He had lost almost all control over his body and remained drowsy throughout. Somehow, I managed to support his frail frame against mine and boarded the flight back to Jammu.

Once back home, soon after he regained some consciousness, he was even more resigned and despondent than before. He again began occupying the same corner of his bed, assuming the same posture with his elbow resting on the bed's headrest and his hand supporting his shiftless head, as he oscillated between contemplating deeply and wailing resoundingly.

On some days, he would ask me to log onto his desktop on the study table in his room and put on his playlist of Bollywood songs from the '60s and '70s. He would specifically ask for the popular Rajesh Khanna song *"Zindagi ke safar mein guzar jaate hain jo makaam, woh phir nahin aate"* to be played on repeat and would sing along in a voice filled with broken sobs.

I, on the other hand, was consumed with guilt. I had offered him a ray of hope to cling on to, only to have it cruelly snatched away from him. I had shown him a dream, and now he was convinced that it would never materialise. I was the one responsible for his suffering. I alone was to blame for inflicting this agony upon him.

He persisted in this state for a week, following our return from Delhi, maintaining his daily routine of dialysis, medications and home treatments; until one day, his condition took a turn for the worse. He began experiencing severe coughing fits and started throwing up whatever little food he was consuming. We admitted him to a private hospital in Jammu.

Throughout my father's illness, I had picked up a lot of medical terms, but "end-life delirium" wasn't a phrase I was familiar with during that time. None of the doctors or nurses ever mentioned it. It wasn't until several years later that I discovered the term and finally understood what was really happening to my Dad.

Of the two weeks that my father was hospitalised in Jammu, he suffered from acute delirium the first week—overwhelmed with extreme restlessness, confusion, paranoia and agitation. Throughout that harrowing period, he would try to make frantic attempts to remove all the IV tubes attached to his body. Wanting to break free, he would violently try to climb out of bed, kicking all four limbs in different directions, screaming and crying as he stared blankly in desperation, "Take me out of here! They are coming for me! They will catch me and kill me!"

I attempted to decipher what he was trying to say; but in all likelihood, his illness, coupled with his anxieties and loss of vision, had left his mind foggy, and the resulting hallucinations had dissociated him from reality. I would try to soothe him, reassuring him that I was there by his side.

He would turn to me, his clouded eyes wide and his eyeballs protruding as far as they possibly could, and shout, "Run! Run away! They will catch you! Run away from here!"

In an attempt to contain his restless movements and prevent him from harming himself with the equipment attached to his body, I would climb onto his bed beside him. Lying by his side, I would grab his wrists with my hands and block his legs with mine to stop him from kicking. All night, for several nights, I wept lying in the same position as he continued to scream.

I was drained—emotionally, physically, mentally.

I didn't have any more vitality left to keep it going, to hold on to the body of my delirious father that had become, surprisingly, much stronger and more aggressive than in the days before.

"I AM NOT SUPPOSED TO DO THIS! PLEASE GOD! HELP ME!" I wanted to scream. I was exhausted, terrified and broken. I was all of that, but mostly, I was alone in my misery, lonely in my wretched reality.

The only saving grace in all of it was that my misery transpired in the seclusion of a ward room with no one to witness the humiliation of our present state, except for the occasional nurse who would show up to check on my dad.

He Died

A week later, my father slipped into a state of complete unconsciousness. The sole visible indication of life within him was that he continued to breathe. His limbs, which had been ceaselessly in motion, kicking and punching until just a few days earlier, had now lost all life.

I remember one particular afternoon clear as day, another day in May that remains etched indelibly in my memory.

I was accompanying my father's stretcher to the MRI room to undergo some scans. As the physician readied him for the scan, an email notification popped up on my phone. It was from the administrative office of a business school.

While in Mumbai, taking inspiration from my roommates, I had begun preparing for higher education, a master's in business studies. Before I embarked on the mission to save my father, I had managed to squeeze in a few interviews for the business schools that had shortlisted me. Although the results were still pending, I had all but forgotten about them in the middle of all the chaos.

The message I had received on my phone was from a college in Gurgaon that was at the top of my list. For months, I had been praying to hear back from them. I quickly browsed through the email's contents. It was a congratulatory note, offering me a spot in their upcoming batch and requesting me to accept the opportunity within the next five days or it would be considered void and offered to the next eligible candidate.

I placed my phone back in my handbag and stared blankly at my father's unconscious body as it slid into the hollow cavity of the MRI machine. I didn't feel a thing, not even a second of jubilation. None of it mattered anymore. My body had shrunk from fatigue and despair, and tears had welled up in my eyes.

More than anything else, more than an admission to a fancy business school, more than the prospect of forging a new life in Mumbai or someplace else, more than any other aspiration I ever had, I only wanted one thing in that moment—for my Dad to be okay.

Out of sheer desperation, I began to bargain with God, "Take all of this away. I don't want to build a new life. I don't want to leave Jammu. I'll return and never leave again. Just make him better. That's all I ask for." Of course, my prayers went unanswered. Perhaps because, as always, they were last minute, and perhaps it was too small a barter that I was offering in lieu of my father's life.

My father stopped responding to all treatment at the end of the second week of his hospitalisation and was soon put on life support. I was informed that water had filled up in his lungs, though I wasn't given the precise details of how that had occurred. I was not permitted to see him, but the doctors declared that he was critical and saving him with his multiple complications had become exceedingly difficult. I promptly started calling my extended family. I could sense that the end was imminent, that there was no hope left.

By the time my family began to arrive, he had already been pronounced dead. I recollect sitting on the hospital corridor floor, immersed in a violent flurry of tears. He was gone—the provider of the family, the force that somehow held the other three of us together, the only one who would call me every day without fail even as I spat relentless vengeance at him.

The one who never said it to me but who, I knew, loved me nonetheless.

I seethed with anger at the universe for the sheer cruelty it had served to my father, for cursing him with a painfully slow and horrendous death and making me a witness to its excruciating details. He didn't deserve to die like this. I didn't deserve to see him go like this. My brother didn't deserve to lose his father this early in his life. We didn't deserve any of it.

Swarms of people began to show up, like they always do in the aftermath. I heard someone call out, "Make sure we remove all valuables from the body."

***

The sofas in our living room were moved to the porch, creating space for my father's body to be placed in the centre for people to pay their respects. He was wrapped entirely in white cloth, only his head exposed. Someone had brought marigold garlands to drape around his neck; a small lit diya sat next to his head.

I observed it all from the entrance of the living room, my tired body leaning against the door.

None of this was of any significance to me now. However, it was quite the spectacle to watch people become overly participative and devoted, now that he was gone. The fervour they showed was markedly lacking when he was still alive and struggling, when there was still a chance to save him.

I had become somewhat accustomed to this well-orchestrated dance of society by the time Abhinav died, but it was all quite new to me when my father passed. It was almost puzzling to watch the conduct of all the people who showed up to see my father. They wept so emotively, so excessively. They wailed as if my father was the only one that mattered to them, as if they couldn't possibly survive a day without him, as if it was the end of the world for them. I continued to observe this charade from a distance.

Then I witnessed something even more bizarre happen. A few middle-aged women, whose faces I couldn't place in my memory, approached my mother, embraced her tightly, and began howling—as if they intimately knew her pain and felt it in the depth of their very bones.

But what was even more astounding to witness was that their howls and cries were met with an equally resounding wail from my mother. Her cries continued to echo across the room as the women embraced her. She, then, proceeded to hug my father, lifting his lifeless upper body from the ground as much as she could. Her cries intensified, echoing even louder.

I was bewildered; her reaction caught me completely off guard. I couldn't help but wonder what it was that pained her exactly, especially when it had been long established that she despised him. Shouldn't she be relieved that her tormentor was gone? Why was she crying? Was it just an act that she had to put on to comply with the expectations of everyone around, and she was such a remarkable actor that I could not catch her bluff? Or did she cry because she could already feel the weight of responsibilities that would fall upon her with Dad's death? Or were her wails really a conduit for the release of two decades of trauma that had been culminating towards this very day and this very moment?

It did not seem like she was faking; from what I had known of my mother for more than twenty years, those were tears of genuine sorrow.

Her reaction made me briefly question the validity of the version of my parents' relationship that I had formed in my mind. Perhaps I was completely deluded; but in that moment, something inside of me wanted to believe that my mother did share a bond with my father, that wasn't founded only on hatred and abuse. I wanted to believe that there were parts of their story that I was unaware of, that there was more to their relationship than what met the eyes.

Maybe the smiles that I had seen in their pictures together, from the few family vacations we took, weren't entirely fake. Perhaps those photographs were tangible proof of fleeting moments of joy that they had shared.

In the vulnerability of the moment and in a last attempt to rescue the memories of their tragic relationship, there was something inside of me that was desperate to believe that it was the remembrance of those traces of her love for my father that drove my mother to tears.

As my chachas hastened to lift my dad's body to take it to the cremation ground, I hurriedly held his head in my palms and whispered a promise softly into his ears, "I will take care of Mummy and Rosu, don't you worry. I promise you. I will." I don't know what it is about me and making grand commitments to the dead, commitments that I never end up fulfilling.

Three days later, I accepted the offer from the business school in Gurgaon; the course was to commence just a fortnight after my dad's death. I was left with no other choice; it was my only way out. I had to escape from my life once again.

Returning to Mumbai was no longer an option. In a state of sheer panic and desperation, I had ended up calling my roommate in Mumbai, wailing, "He died! I couldn't save him! I did this to him!" Just like that, I had ended up violating the sacredness of Mumbai as my two realities ceased to exist separately. I couldn't leave my misery behind in Jammu anymore; I knew I would find it patiently waiting for me in Mumbai as well.

Staying in Jammu wasn't an option either. I was certain that all hell would break loose after my father's death. I had to escape once more, to a place where

I could be a stranger yet again, where I could perhaps forge a future from scratch once again. One more time, perhaps for one last time.

While I weaved this future in Gurgaon and my mother withdrew further into her own being, all the brunt of what ensued was borne by my brother. I failed to shield him as I had so valiantly promised to my dying father.

In inheritance from our father, my brother got the disputes, the anxieties and the anger that continued to linger on even after our father's death. Freshly graduated at the time, he had planned to stay at home a few months before embarking on a job search. But as those months turned into years, he found himself entangled in escalating family feuds. Meanwhile, I kept away, immersing myself into the busy routines of business school. While I was tormented by the trauma preceding my father's death, I let my brother be tormented by the realities that emerged in its aftermath.

I failed to protect him and my mother from what had become a house of both mental as well as physical illness, especially as the health of my chachas also gradually grew worse. To save my own sanity, I allowed both of them to languish instead.

24

Death all Around, Everywhere

My father's death triggered a series of bizarre events in our family; something truly unbelievable began to happen. It marked the beginning of an end that we could have never foreseen, an end that violently shook the lives of all sixteen people who lived under the roof of my grandfather's wretched house.

Six months after my Dad's death, my elder chacha succumbed to a heart attack. Two months after that tragedy, my younger chacha passed away from a kidney complication similar to my father's.

No one could fathom what was happening; we were stupefied as much as we were traumatised. We were collapsing like little pieces of dominoes, one after another, under the piling weight of the other dominoes. It seemed as if the siblings who had grown up holding each other's hands couldn't bear to continue living without one another, despite all the hatred that spewed among them in their final years. Each of them, as they departed, seemed to be beckoning the younger one to join him in the other world, in the same sequence as they had arrived in this one.

I was travelling to Jammu from my college every few months, making up excuses for why I needed to be home urgently, too ashamed to reveal the truth. I watched my chachas' bodies, one after the other, shrouded tightly in white cloth as they lay on the floor of the same living room where my father did. I stood in the same cemetery, over and over again, as the dense black smoke from the burning pyres choked and killed me a little more every time. I watched my younger cousins wail for the loss of their fathers and, as I held on to their quivering hands, not a single tear fell from my eyes.

My body was numb and stoic in the face of this never-ending onslaught of tragedy, the astonishment of each passing moment being more ludicrous than the last. "Please stop this, God! Please end this!" I screamed to the invisible powers of the universe as my world slowly crumbled, piece by piece.

We became the talk of the town, a family whose entire generation had been wiped away in the span of a year in a series of unrelated events. Rumours began circulating, speculating everything from black magic to a curse on the house. Maybe the house was indeed cursed; maybe *all* of us were cursed; maybe one of us who was cursed had brought all this misfortune upon everyone else; maybe that one person was me.

I would often find myself battling the validity of it all. Had it truly transpired, or was it a fabrication of my mind? Was it real, or was it merely a series of nightmares I had just woken up from? The events were so outlandish that I assumed nobody would ever believe them, so much so that I never dared to bring them up with anyone outside my family.

Occasionally, when I could muster the courage to recount and narrate to a friend what had happened, it would sound so nonsensical in my mind that I would begin to fumble for words and halt mid-sentence. It seemed excessively laborious to explain the hows, whats and whys of the whole thing.

I was ashamed of it all—the deaths and the ensuing misery. Even if some of my friends were aware of my father's death, I dreaded the possibility of them learning about my chachas. I didn't want to punish them and burden them with the devastating reality that we lived in. They couldn't possibly handle it.

As destiny continued to strike us over and over again, ironically, it was me who was mortified of what it had served us, when it should clearly have been the gods above. It was the shame of those gods; the gods who continued to torment us endlessly, the gods who seemed to show no mercy whatsoever.

It was the shame of the gods above.

We spend our lives trying to hide from our past; we run like we can outrun it. Breathless in our attempt to escape from it, we sprint with mindless devotion, until one day, we can no longer run away from it. Because that very past, sooner or later, catches up and becomes who we are.

And just like that, we are exposed, stripped naked in front of the entire world. They see us for what we are—imposters, trying to be one of them. They see us for who we really are.

25

The Two Main Men

Life, I grew up believing, was supposed to be an upward-moving graph. Sure, there were going to be occasional plummets and prolonged troughs. But I remained, for the longest time, tirelessly optimistic that it would all work out in the end.

However, with Abhinav's death, I started to see myself as a tragic exception to this graph—instead of troughs and peaks, I was stuck in a continuum of concentric circles of misery that I couldn't break away from.

My father took his last breath on May 16, 2014. As fate would have it, Abhinav was admitted in the hospital on May 11, seven years later, and his health had started deteriorating by May 13. As the ominous date of May 16 loomed once again, I found myself filled with dread. All the memories and trauma of my father's death, which I had desperately tried to forget over the years, resurfaced with a jolt. As I went through the motions of talking to doctors about treatments and medicines, I was stricken with irrepressible anxiety and fear.

I was somehow convinced that all Abhinav had to do to live was simply make it past May 16. It was as though the date stood in the Grim Reaper's stead, that had come to collect from me what I cherished most. All I had to do was pull my husband away from its deep claws and things would return to as they were.

May 16, 2021, eventually did arrive and pass and I sighed in relief, certain that things would take a turn for the better, but they never did. The demon was cunning; it lingered patiently for eight more days and took what it had come for.

I, in a sickening turn of events, was living the same truth twice, seven years and eight days apart. Life was perhaps just running in circles and it had run a full circle in that time. I was way too deluded, thinking that I was moving away and forward from what had happened, but in reality, I was slowly moving towards it again.

***

Every now and then, I catch myself unintentionally comparing the deaths of my father and my husband, even though the relationships I had shared with them were vastly different and their deaths had occurred almost a decade apart.

My mind perceives the two tragedies as events unfolding simultaneously in two parallel universes. For reasons unknown to me, it keeps attempting to arrive at a "weighted average grief," rating various aspects of loss in each case— the acceptance, the anger, the amount I miss them. Which death was more agonising for the person who died? Which one caused *me* more agony? Which death was more unfair to them and which was more unfair to me?

The acceptance of the two losses varied.

While Dad's decline, dragging out over two years, was distressing to witness for the torment it caused, acceptance of his death had come easier. In fact, it had felt like a weight had been lifted, both from him and me. Although the memories of the events leading up to his death kept me traumatised for a long time, I soon began to see his death and the deaths of my chachas as our family's rock bottom. Things could only get better from here.

But, when Abhinav died a year into our marriage, it demolished me beyond all reason and meaning. It was a rock bottom to my original rock bottom, a rock bottom that I didn't think could exist. My belief that life was supposed to be a zero-sum game—that all suffering and all joy must eventually cancel each other out in this very lifetime was shattered into a million little pieces.

While my dad's death felt like a pause, Abhinav's death was a full stop. I was so disoriented and clueless, I lost all will to carry on. What is the point of the hustling, the jostling, the struggling to rise again when I am going to end up with an even more monumental tragedy anyway? Why bother rebuilding my life when I have no control over it, when I will invariably be struck by destiny again?

The grieving of the two losses varied.

I never really fully grieved my father's death until Abhinav died. Immediately after my father's passing, I threw myself into an ocean of overstimulation at business school, where living from class to class and semester to semester didn't leave me any time to absorb and process what had transpired in the past few months.

The sole coping mechanism I had adopted to deal with my loss and loneliness of my loss was donning a vest of resilience. "Nothing can break me," "I will emerge from it stronger than ever," "I will not shed a tear," were my survival mantras. Being strong and suppressing my grief seemed like the only viable way out.

While sitting in my class, during presentations, while in the cafeteria, I constantly teetered on the edge of exploding into a torrent of tears. Yet, the dread of being labelled weak, a loser, a whiner, was so immense that it kept me from breaking down.

The little grieving I did manage to do was limited to staring blankly at my father's wallet-sized picture that I had carefully tucked away in a folder alongside some important documents. In the solitude of my dorm room, I would sit on my bed, clutching on to his photo; meticulously examining the details of his face, only to discover new contours that had previously escaped my notice.

But, with Abhinav's death, I couldn't pretend to be strong anymore. There was a deluge of emotions, old and new, that my body could no longer hold in anymore. The grief that had been bottled up for years, along with the new, freshly brewed grief, mercilessly demolished the walls of restraint and compliance, and came gushing out, like a valiant warrior ready to shatter my entire existence.

But the fear of forgetting them was the same...

As the days, months and years went by following my Dad's death, I thought less and less about him. Most recently, I had fondly remembered him when Abhinav and I began contemplating getting married. In those days, I had often wondered what it would have been like to introduce Abhinav to my Dad. Would the two have hit it off? Would my Dad have approved of Abhinav?

It would have been quite an interesting interaction to witness between the two main men of my life. I could picture Abhinav being his usual charming self, and his chattiness being met with the initial smugness of my dad. Yet soon enough, Dad's demeanour would have softened, eventually showering Abhinav with all his subtle affection as an extension of his love for me.

My memories of my father, over the years, have grown sparse. I remember how terrified I was of him in my early years, how much in pain he was during his last days. But unfortunately, those are the only fragments of his life that my mind chooses to selectively preserve.

I do remember some of his other peculiarities—like his love for singing. He loved singing at the top of his voice when he was alone in his room. He was a music enthusiast of sorts, though his singing abilities didn't quite match up to his love for it. Regardless of what the song was, he would always sing it in a specific rhythm, with no regard for the original melody.

Annoyed by this loud and off-key singing, I would often walk up to his room to correct him, "The lyrics are right, but that's not how the song goes." I'd proceed to demonstrate a somewhat better rendition of the song. Yet, he would persist, continuing to sing in his unique manner. Despite the frustration I felt at this, his tactics would bring a wry grin to my face.

But other than that, I remember little of what my father was outside of his illness.

Which is why when I lost Abhinav, an acute fear gripped me—that he would soon fade into obscurity just like my Dad. That his friends and his family would gradually move on and conversations about him would become rarer. Scarier than that was the possibility that I, of all people, would forget him— that five, ten, twenty years down the line, he would remain a blurry memory, remembered only on birthdays and anniversaries.

Or even worse—the tormenting memories of those fifteen harrowing days in the hospital would overshadow all the good times we spent together.

Of course, there were things about him that I will never forget, not in a million lifetimes. I will never forget how puffy his eyes would be in the mornings, how I would attempt to open them using my thumb and index finger, how that would make him chuckle. I will never forget the fascination I felt as I held his hands into mine, his uniquely long fingers, and their flat tips. I will never forget his dense, soft hair, and how I used to envy those luscious curls. I will never forget the scar on his right foot, a mark from a freak accident from when he was three years old. Although it no longer hurt him, I found a strange comfort in occasionally running my finger over it, believing it was soothing to him.

I knew it would take me more than my mortality to forget any of that. I knew I would spot the unique sparkle of his eyes a hundred years from now, from a thousand miles away.

But for everything else, I needed a system.

I had to meticulously devise a plan to ensure that Abhinav wouldn't fade out of my present as life moved on. I had to keep him alive, at least till the time I was alive. I started brainstorming for ways to achieve that.

To begin with, I filled our home with dozens of pictures of us, scattered throughout the bedroom and living room. Some framed, many unframed. Some were placed on tables, others were hung on walls and a few were pinned to the memory board atop my work desk.

Then, I began, very consciously, inserting him in conversations with friends and family, to ensure that we kept talking about him and he remained the centre of our world. I would reach out to his friends on an impulse, eager to know more about him from people who had known him long before I did. Perhaps I creeped a few of them out in the process.

But none of it was sustainable.

Then, a truly brilliant idea struck me. I started to maintain a little black diary where I began meticulously jotting down every single memory of Abhinav that I could summon. I wanted to capture it all while it was still vivid, before it started to become hazy.

I wrote about how he looked and the little details of his body that were so uniquely his. I put down the jokes he used to tell—not that there were many— and despite my obvious irritation, he would recycle them over and over again, and then chuckle with pride at his supposed exceptional sense of humour. I wrote about what he loved to eat and how he ate it. I wrote down every intricate detail that I could remember and categorised them into sections: "Our First Meeting" "Abhinav's Favourite Shows" "Our Jokes" "Our First Trip."

I didn't keep the diary in plain sight. I kept it hidden in a box, something akin to a "box of memories" as if I was a brooding teenager going through her first heartbreak. Alongside the diary, I stored handwritten letters he had penned during our courtship, some addressed "To my Senior Consultant," in the box. I stored some dried petals of flowers that I had received from him, as well as all the endearing little cards and gifts.

I rarely open the box now, fearing the emotional turmoil that its contents might cause. I open it when a memory that I have not documented comes to me, and I hastily reach for my diary to preserve it before it slips away entirely.

I open the box on days I miss him so terribly that I can't resist myself from opening it. I open it once in a while to cry and laugh, simultaneously, remembering and yearning for the joyful days of the past.

Despite all this effort, nothing I did ever felt enough. With each passing day, I was still drifting further away from Abhinav, however much I tried not to. His existence had been reduced to fine grains of sand, and the harder I tried to grasp them, the more they seemed to slip through my fingertips.

Part V

Months After

26

Always a Loner

They want you to repress the pain and bury it in the recesses of your hearts, insisting that is what is rational, that is what will help you survive the waves of grief that have so suddenly and so ferociously hit you—you must force that pain so deep down that it could never find its way out to agitate you again.

Days turned into weeks, weeks into months as I found myself in the midst of friends, family and strangers who urged me constantly: to get better soon, move on, be strong, not feel "sad anymore."

But sadness was all that I had left of Abhinav. I couldn't just let go of it. I wanted to feel it in every fibre of my being; I wanted it to permeate into my bones, course through the very last drop of blood in my body and take complete control of me.

I knew that even if I attempted to repress any part of it, it would just not vanish. Instead, it would thrive and bloom and poison the insides of my body like a toxic weed from the wild.

They kept insisting—surround yourself with friends and family; it will comfort you. Yet, my immediate instinct was to distance myself from everyone—no one understood my pain. I wanted to escape to a faraway place where there would be no one to belittle my suffering, where I would not be required to comply with the *definition* and the *magnitude* that others had assigned to my loss.

People and their words became white noise, faint murmurs in the background of the loud chatter in my head—of me questioning God, holding my dad responsible for not saving my husband and confronting Abhinav for abandoning me. Amidst that internal dialogue, my reality had ceased to exist on the outside and taken root entirely inside of my mind.

This inner reality felt much more tangible than the world outside. People were mere moving and talking objects whom I couldn't relate to anymore, just as they couldn't relate to me anymore. They talked to me, but whatever they said somehow didn't seem to penetrate my consciousness anymore. All their words drowned at a distance away from me.

I desired complete and eternal solitude to fully embrace my inner world, to make sense of all the turmoil in my heart and the clamour in my head. I resolved to be alone because that is what the gods above had destined for me; Abhinav's death was the last but very clear intimation that they wanted me to suffer alone. If that is what the divine will was, then I was prepared to comply. I wouldn't resist anymore.

I decided to leave Abhinav's parents home in Delhi and return to Gurgaon in August 2021.

***

At Abhinav's parents' home, everything still felt...temporary, as if Abhinav wasn't really dead—he was at the office, or he was at our Gurgaon home— anywhere but gone from this world. But upon returning to our own home, the clarity of his absence hit me with all its force. This was real, and not just a nightmare I could simply wake up from any moment.

The house was a disaster site, a physical manifestation of what my life was at the moment. Newspapers collected over weeks were scattered all over the muddied balcony; many were soggy from the rains and were rotting. Our once-vibrant house plants had all withered away. Several layers of dust had settled over the furniture in our living room. Fresh seepage damage adorned our bedroom wall, emanating a damp, pungent odour that reached every corner of the house. Vegetables in the fridge that I had forgotten to take out while leaving in a rush were now rotting with mould.

But it was not this mess that grabbed my attention first. It was the collision of Abhinav's presence and absence, the moment I entered the house, that knocked the wind out of me. I saw him everywhere—on the sofa in our living room where we had our movie nights, in the kitchen where he made breakfast daily, in our bedroom, engrossed in a book, waiting patiently as I dealt with work calls, gesturing at his watch now and then. He was everywhere.

Every little thing was a memory of how it had come into existence by us coming together, how he had touched it, how he had talked about it. It was a reminder that *we* had existed—it was not just a dream I had fantasised about, but a life that we had lived.

The unopened packet of a new brand of coffee that he had recently bought to try lay on the kitchen counter. The black sports jacket that I had gifted him for his birthday, tags still on, sat in the cupboard. His towel and night suit hung in our bathroom. His clothes, ironed, lay neatly arranged in his wardrobe. His shoes stood lined up perfectly with mine on the shoe rack. Everything was exactly where it used to be, staring at me in disbelief—How could he be gone? He is all over here.

I stared back, blankly, at all our possessions, each one so painstakingly selected and bought only a few months ago. So much effort, time, deliberation, guidance from Mom and Papa had gone into it all; just to ensure that the washing machine, the sofa, the bed, the curtains will last us three, five, ten years.

But for what? Why did we go through all that trouble if it was all going to end this soon; when *we* weren't going to last for even two full years? All of it felt so pointless.

I picked up the pieces of our house and my life and cried in the empty rooms. I cried while taking showers. I cried while cooking for myself. I cried while binge-watching *The Mindy Project*. I cried during work Zoom meetings with my camera off and my microphone muted. I would cry until I exhausted myself, and then I would go back to my daily commitments. But soon enough, I'd start crying again.

My need to talk to Abhinav, to touch him, to feel his presence was interminable. In his absence, I wanted to perish—much like our house plants that had gradually withered away over weeks, in the absence of water and light: so quietly, so effortlessly, without being a nuisance to anyone.

It was appalling, the incredible loneliness I felt for the very first time in my life. It made no logical sense that so easily and so quickly, I had un-learned how to live and survive by myself.

Before Abhinav, I had long considered myself a loner, often taking pride in my emotional and physical self-sufficiency. Then why, all of a sudden, had my life become so directionless without this one person? Why was it so incredibly difficult? How could Abhinav have undone all the self-reliance that I had cultivated over a period of thirty years in such a short time? I was furious at him—and myself—for becoming so dependent on him for my survival. So much so that I couldn't even breathe without him, that there were nights when I would find myself waking up and hyperventilating.

The kind of trivial things that would trigger me were beyond astonishing. On one occasion, as I was leaving for work, I forgot my keys and found myself locked outside the apartment. I sat on the stairs, sobbing for a whole hour, aggravated because now I would have to remember to carry my keys, every time I left home. In the past, I could afford to forget them; Abhinav would always have a spare set. Other times, I would unexpectedly burst into tears while carrying my own luggage to and from the airport.

Also for the first time, I was terribly terrified to be alone in our home. The house which had once been filled with cheerful voices and chatter, of Abhinav singing, of the both of us laughing, of music playing, was suddenly consumed by a strange, eerie silence.

I had lived by myself before, but never in such absolute solitude and carrying such absolute pain.

My heart would start pounding at the slightest unrecognisable noise at night. Eyes wide open, I would sit at the edge of my bed and wait for something unexpected to happen. When, after fifteen minutes or so, nobody would have jumped out of the curtains to stab me, I would break down—again—in uncontrollable sobs, acutely aware of my slow descent into insanity. I soon began sleeping with my bedroom locked, with a kitchen knife and pepper spray on my bed stand. Weeks would pass before I began to feel at ease in the house again. Strangely, the eeriness became the source of my peace now.

****

Once I began to feel a bit more settled in the house, I took up the Herculean task of deciding the fate of Abhinav's belongings: his clothes, his shoes, his watches, his perfumes and his elaborate grooming kit that now sat abandoned in the washroom.

I could have tackled it all after a few months, but I was consumed by a sense of urgency to decide what needed to be done with them—what had to be donated, what could be kept as a memory, what Papa could use and what I could keep for my own use. Perhaps a part of me wanted to quickly rip off the bandage while the wound was still afresh, feel all the pain that I had to, and get on with life.

Papa, thankfully, offered to come to Gurgaon to help me with the task.

Even as his wife, it felt such a breach of Abhinav's privacy to go through his belongings without him. It felt absolutely, irrationally wrong. What if he comes back? What if he demands his favourite shirt? What will I say to him?

I saw tears welling up in Papa's eyes as he set aside a few of Abhinav's clothes for his own use, a pair of running shoes that Papa still uses for his morning walks and some t-shirts and jackets that fitted him.

I set aside a few things that I couldn't bear to part with, like the black Deadpool t-shirt that said, "This is What Awesomeness Looks Like," which I had gifted to him a few weeks into dating. *Deadpool* was the first movie we had watched together. I also kept his favourite blue polo tee. In all my recent dreams about him, he would always be wearing that t-shirt. I kept the iconic bathrobe he loved to roam around in on weekends. I kept all his perfumes, which I would occasionally open to catch a whiff of, just to remind myself what he used to smell like.

We were wrapping up his life, one belonging at a time, without his permission.

Slowly, all his belongings would either perish or would be stored away in boxes. Slowly, his presence would start becoming less and less prominent in the way that I lived my life. And years later, there would come a day when there would be absolutely nothing in my house that would have touched him.

27

Vanishing

Nobody really calls you a "widow" to your face; at least no one did to me. They likely use the term when they talk about you to others.

That it's a label that would now be attached to me didn't dawn on me for quite some time. It managed to creep into my life in the form of a dozen or more documents that needed to be filled out following Abhinav's death—for banks, for provident fund accounts, for insurance and a whole list of endless things. Each document I filled out was a cruel reminder that—I was thirty-two and widowed. I found myself marking the "widow of the deceased" box on these documents and penning letters signed as "declaration by the widow" every other day in the initial months. My hand, and the pen in it, would quiver every time that I was asked to do that.

I couldn't help but wonder that if I never remarried, would I forever carry that label, or if, at some point, I would naturalise back to being "single," perhaps ten, twenty, thirty years down the line? I wondered what that timeline was, or if there was a timeline at all.

The most excruciating part of filling these documents, without a doubt, was having to attach a copy of my husband's death certificate. I remember the exact moment when Papa first handed over the certificate and a few photocopies to me, instructing me to file them securely. My heart had sunk. It felt as if a death sentence had been handed to me.

Name of the deceased: Abhinav Agrawal

Name of spouse: Minerva Khajuria

Date of death: May 24, 2021

Location of death: So and so hospital

But a few months in, I grew accustomed to it all. With dozens of copies of Abhinav's death certificate lying scattered throughout our home, it had become one of the many documents that came to affirm my identity.

And soon enough, the label of "widow" didn't repulse me anymore either. In fact, "Widowed" had become an easier option to choose on forms. What proved more confusing to fill were the forms that didn't include a "Widowed" option to indicate marital status. My hand would hover as I struggled to choose between "Married" and "Single."

I was "Married" because I had married a man a year-and-a-half ago. Although he had died, we weren't really separated or divorced. We were still very much married to each other. But simultaneously, I was also technically "Single," because the person I was married to didn't exist anymore.

The ambiguity of my relationship status had never been so perplexing. "Are you married?" ceased to be a simple yes or no question. It was now a lump in the throat and a tear in the eye; it was now a trigger to an internal debate—to tell or not to tell.

I ended up marking myself "Married" on some forms and "Single" on others, leaning slightly more towards "Married" because I liked the ring of it, and also because choosing "Single" felt like a deceit, as if I was being unfaithful to Abhinav, as if I was erasing our entire history together. While I made these choices, I crossed my fingers, hoping my whims wouldn't lead to any discrepancies in the official records.

***

As the spread of COVID-19 began to slow down and the world cautiously ventured out again, some of my friends suggested we meet up. The thought of agreeing to the plans felt extremely burdensome, so I resorted to making excuses.

The primary reason for it was that I felt like a failure and looked like one. While brushing my teeth or washing my face, standing before the bathroom mirror, I started becoming aware of how much I had aged in a matter of months. I noticed the wrinkles around my eyes, on my neck and lining my mouth. A massive acne cyst had stubbornly been sitting on my chin for months now. My eyes were perpetually swollen from the relentless crying, and huge, dark bags had appeared beneath them. I had always had more grey hair than an average 30-year-old (something I'd inherited from my mom) but suddenly, it felt as though my entire head had turned white. I had shed a significant amount of weight during the initial months following Abhinav's death, only to gain even more subsequently.

My trauma was not just manifesting in my mind, it had also been scarring my body. As I gazed at the fatigued person staring back at me in the mirror, I couldn't believe it was me. I couldn't reconcile this image with the person whose vibrant pictures, dated just a few months back, were stored in the gallery of my phone. She was a stranger with whom I saw no resemblance.

I was ashamed of how I looked. I was ashamed of the series of deaths in my family, and I was ashamed of the misery that consumed me. I was ashamed of my life all over again. I was ashamed, when clearly it should have been the gods above.

The sense of shame was so crippling that I didn't return to Jammu for over a year after Abhinav's death. I wanted to avoid everyone and their pity. I wanted to spare myself the awkward glances, the superficial conversations, their struggle of thinking the right words to say, when there weren't going to be any.

Spending countless hours alone at home, I found my thoughts drifting frequently to a girl I knew in school. She and I had shared the same class for several years. Though we weren't close, we did have several mutual friends. I was even invited to her birthday parties on a few occasions.

We were in the tenth grade when I heard that she lost her father. She continued to attend school thereafter, but appeared distant and withdrawn. I couldn't recall having any interactions with her following that. She seemed inaccessible, and I, too, felt hesitant to approach someone when I didn't know what to say.

A few months later, there was even more distressing news. Tragically, and quite unbelievably, her brother had also passed away. I wasn't sure of the reasons behind the two deaths, and I didn't make any effort to investigate further.

Then, a few weeks later, she simply disappeared, as if into thin air. I never crossed paths with her again, neither at school nor outside. Several rumours about what happened to her made the rounds. Among those speculations,

I heard that her family had consulted a pandit after the deaths and that he had advised them to never marry her off, for it would bring more misfortune to their family. Her story was devastating as it was, and this prophecy from the priest seemed extremely unfair.

In the years that followed, I often found myself thinking about her because on the way from the Jammu railway station to my home, stood a hotel that belonged to her family. It was an imposing building, impossible to miss.

Every time my eyes would fall on that massive structure, I would think of her. I would reminisce about the time she invited us there for a birthday celebration. She had reserved a room and arranged room service for all of us. It was all very fancy, with the pristine white hotel linens and the gleaming porcelain crockery. It remains one of the most memorable birthday parties I have ever attended.

But now, the hotel looked abandoned and forlorn, shattered from the outside. None of the rooms were ever lit up, and several had broken windows. Every once in a while, when I couldn't get her out of my mind and couldn't stop thinking about what had happened to her, I would impulsively search the internet, hoping to find a trace of her.

Unfortunately, all I ever found was news about the hotel shutting down due to legal disputes within the family over ownership. That was all. I failed to find anything more. She was nowhere—not on Facebook, LinkedIn, Instagram. She had disappeared from the face of the earth, just like that.

After Abhinav's death, I thought about her even more, and my attempts to locate her became even more desperate. I wanted to know what had happened to her because I believed that my own destiny had brought me to the very crossroads where she had once stood. I desperately wanted to know how her life had turned out following those storms, because I began to believe that her journey and mine were connected somehow, and that whatever happened to her *then* would define what would happen to me *now*. I scoured the internet tirelessly, but my efforts yielded nothing.

I wondered what it was about death and tragedy that made people vanish into oblivion like that. Were they frightened to confront the world after their tragedy? Or was it, in fact, the other way around—that the world was petrified of them?

Perhaps this unease stemmed from the fact that for most people, death remains a truth somewhere far away in a distant future; a truth that is a lie at least for the foreseeable time; a truth which is true for others but not for them, until inevitably, sooner or later, it does become an undeniable truth for each and every one of us.

But until then, they choose to blissfully deny it, pretending to be oblivious to its existence.

And then there is us, people like me and the girl from my school, who find themselves becoming the living embodiments of death. Facing us perhaps scares the rest of the world because it makes the mythical concept of death more real to them, forcing them to question their own mortality and the mortality of their loved ones. If it could happen to us, it could happen to them.

And so they subtly nudge us to fade into the background with statements like, "You will lose everyone if you are going to be sad like this," "No one wants to be around depressed people," "Let's talk about something else."

For the rest of them to continue living this comforting lie, to keep their zest for life intact, people like that girl from my school just evaporate into thin air; maybe that was what was destined for me as well.

I found myself rooting for her, wherever she was. I wanted to stumble upon something, some clue, some indication that her life had turned out fine. I desperately hoped that she was out there, living a life that was not marred by death and misery. I wanted her to have triumphed over her trauma, in the hope that I could triumph over mine as well.

28

How to be a Widow

The fear of fading into obscurity was paralysing. I couldn't allow myself to vanish like that; I couldn't let the world write me off so easily.

In an attempt to revive my social life, I gathered all the courage that I could and decided to say yes to a few gatherings.

When I eventually started venturing out after months of lockdown, my first daunting task was to figure out how to play this new role that I suddenly found myself in. It was a much simpler question to answer a year ago. How I needed to dress myself as a newly married Hindu woman was sufficiently clear to me. I understood that in her first year of marriage, a woman was supposed to adorn herself in jewellery, including heavy bangles and earrings. Bright lipstick, bindi and mangalsutra were newlywed essentials. At times, I looked a bit gaudy and ludicrous, dolled up like that, but I thoroughly enjoyed playing the part and would often ask Abhinav to take pictures of me.

But now, as a modern day widow in her early thirties, there was no rulebook on how to look the part. I did not have a clear image of a thirty-something widow in my mind.

Now that I think about it, that's not entirely true, though. I did know a woman in my extended family in Jammu who had lost her husband around the same age as me. For years, I saw her wearing salwar suits in dull colours with a dupatta wrapped around her head as a sign of mourning and modesty. Of course, I was fortunate enough to dwell in a much more progressive environment where I didn't have to emulate her example. There were no prescribed rules, no sets of dos and don'ts that I was aware of, nor did Abhinav's family impose any such customs on me.

So I kept wondering. My extended contemplation was driven by my resolve to mourn the death of my husband in the same visible way that I had celebrated my marriage to him, with the bangles and the bindis and the mangalsutra. But I also wanted to mourn him in a way that would not compromise my pride and self-esteem. Striking the right balance between my love for my deceased husband and upholding my feminist principles through my guise and conduct kept me puzzling over this conundrum.

I also felt a little vulnerable, fearing the judgemental eye of others. Am I dressing up too jovially, or am I dressed too sombrely? What was the right balance? What was the appropriate amount of grief I should signal through my appearance, regardless of the quantum of grief in my heart?

Once again, I found myself turning to the internet to seek examples. I searched Instagram for #widowed, #youngandwidowed, #widowedat30 to find women who could inspire me, who could teach me how to be a widow in my thirties.

Unfortunately, all I found was young American women running grief support pages, offering recovery courses, posting snippets of their breakdowns, snapshots of their happy days and words of motivation for others. There were a few Indian women-run pages as well, celebrating women who were thriving and creating content about how they overcame their trauma.

Then there was Mandira Bedi, an Indian actress and TV presenter, who had recently been widowed too. She had lost her husband a month after I lost Abhinav, but she seemed to be doing so much better than me.

She was, you could say, killing it with her workouts and social appearances, while I struggled to get out of bed every day. Instead of getting inspired, I felt a piercing pang of betrayal watching her. Deep down, I was convinced that she was as tormented as I was, but then why was she masking it? Why was she not revealing her authentic broken self?

Perhaps she couldn't afford to go on a rampage like me; she didn't have the privilege of being a nobody like I did. Being a public figure came with significant social responsibilities, and any major display of distress may have been destructive for her career.

Since there wasn't anything concrete out there, after much browsing and drawing inspiration from a variety of sources, I decided to create my own set of rules for mourning Abhinav's death through my guise.

When it came to makeup, I opted to keep it simple and limited to applying kajal to my eyes. I couldn't possibly skip kajal; without it, my eyes looked like I hadn't slept for ages.

I decided to refrain from wearing lipstick for at least a year.

I also decided to avoid wearing any vibrant clothing for the same period.

Additionally, I noticed that some widows on the internet were wearing their husbands' engagement rings around their necks strung in gold chains, and I began doing the same. I found it to be such a good way of reminding myself of my connection with Abhinav.

When it came to finally facing people, it didn't turn out to be as terrifying or awkward as I had anticipated. Friends and colleagues, whom I was meeting after several months, were genuinely kind to me. Some of them mentioned that they had wanted to reach out but didn't know how, an excuse which, by then, I had calmed down enough to understand and accept.

To my astonishment, all the scenarios that I had concocted in my mind, around my interactions with people as a widow, turned out to be exaggerated. None of them were judgmental of my appearance; none of them looked down at me with pity. It became evident that I had been projecting my own inner inadequacies and vulnerabilities all this while. I had assigned myself too much significance in other people's lives. In reality, everyone was so caught up in their own day-to-day conundrums that my tragedy was merely a passing thought to most of them.

However, what was most astonishing to witness was how the pandemic that had decimated my life was just a minor glitch in theirs.

They did complain about it—about not being able to travel, the challenges of being confined at home with family, having to cook and clean without their household help. But barring that, things were more or less back to business for them.

They discussed the prospect of switching jobs as the markets were booming. They talked about considering relocating out of India, as many others were doing. They even spoke about starting to plan for kids, given that we were all well into our thirties.

Meanwhile, all I could think of was how none of this was relevant to my life anymore. How far behind I had fallen in this race. I smiled and pretended to listen to all their dreams and aspirations for their short-term and the long-term futures. I had nothing to add to those conversations.

The gulf of dissimilarity between me and them had grown wider; my frame of reference had moved much further away from theirs.

I looked at their smiling, innocuous faces, so vibrant, so unscathed by life. How marvellous it must be to lead such a life; a life that is filled with its share of ups and downs, but not to the extent of irreconcilable, unrelenting damage. How glorious it must be to live without the immense baggage of the past and the prospective emptiness of the future. How wonderful it must be to not know death so up and close.

In that moment amidst them all, I didn't yearn to have children, better job opportunities or the prospect of moving to another country. Instead, I wished for the blissful ignorance of how punishing life could be, that glistened in their eyes and mocked me unknowingly.

***

While I met my friends and acquaintances only once in a while, I continued to pay regular visits to Abhinav's parents.

They would always be thrilled when I would announce my arrival. Mom would want to know, "What should I cook for you? Anything special you want to have?" just as she used to ask Abhinav. He would have always had a ready answer for her: pav bhaji, chhole bhature or hakka noodles. In fact, he would start monitoring his diet days in advance, saving all the calories for the sumptuous meals that awaited him at his home.

I, on the other hand, would just respond, exasperated, "Nothing, I don't want anything special. I will eat what everyone else is having."

Papa started waiting for my arrivals downstairs, outside the main gate of their house, prepared to help carry my luggage up to their floor, much as he did for Abhinav. He would always come down to help Abhinav park his car in the haphazard parking spots in their locality.

But I would sternly refuse that too. I would stop him from carrying my bags, "I will take them up myself." I would be adamant.

Their conduct enraged me. It frustrated me that they didn't understand that things were not the same, now that Abhinav was dead. Why are they trying so hard to pretend as if everything is normal? Why are they not angrier? Why are they trying to replicate the relationship they had with Abhinav with me?

I couldn't be Abhinav's proxy for them. I couldn't allow them that luxury. If no one else could be Abhinav for me, I couldn't be Abhinav for them. I couldn't let them have that peace. This had to be equally punishing for everyone involved.

My every visit, without fail, would be marked by several outbursts of explosive rage. I was live ammunition, ready to detonate anytime without any warning, "You don't understand my pain, nobody does! It is killing me! My life is over! You both are in such a rush to forget everything!"

I was behaving like a teenager, demanding everyone's attention to my pain. I had all this pent up rage inside of me with no one to direct it towards, and Abhinav's parents became easy targets; the only people who still tolerated my hysteria. In a way, I was testing their breaking point to see how much more they could endure of me.

My bouts of hysterical outbursts would invariably be followed by pangs of guilt and fear. Guilt, because I was reminded of how this loss was not exclusively mine but equally theirs. And fear, because what if one day they grew tired of all my antics and decided not to tolerate them any longer? I was not a five-year-old; nor was I their own flesh and blood, so why should they indulge my madness?

I was just the woman who was married to their now-dead son, who showed up at their doorstep every few weeks. And as they tried to grieve their son in peace, she would wreak havoc in their already tormented lives. What if, one day, they decided not to answer the door for me anymore?

I couldn't let that happen. While I wished to shut everyone out of my life, including them, I couldn't really let go of them absolutely. They were the only ones who were the living proof of the fact that Abhinav and I had existed. They were a relation I had formed because of Abhinav, the relation which, despite all my tantrums, still somehow persisted. If I lose them, I will lose Abhinav completely and permanently. And I couldn't let that happen.

29

Becoming my Mother

Months later, with COVID-19 restrictions further easing, my brother finally made the trip to visit me in Gurgaon. It had been more than a year since I had last seen him. He brought our mother along.

They were not even past my doorstep when I all but ran to embrace my mother.

I'm not sure why I did that; we don't usually hug. It was an instinctive movement of my arms, perhaps a reflex action driven by the angst of the past few months. A part of me was hopeful that the recent trials and tribulations of my life would have brought a change in my mother—perhaps she would at last look outside her own trauma and into mine. I was hopeful that she might have somehow magically learned to hug me back and say something comforting to her daughter in distress.

But my hope was short-lived. As I hugged her, my mother stood motionless, her arms hanging by her side, her face instinctively jerking away from mine in response to my embrace. I stepped away from her almost immediately, feeling the humiliation and rejection of all the bygone years at once.

Somewhere deep down, in all my rationality and my understanding of her history, I knew that this would be her reaction. I knew that her own trauma had forever changed her and that it was foolish of me to expect anything else from her. But my own loss had made me irrational too, and I was, once again, longing for the mother I never had.

All the pent-up anger and decades of neglect and unworthiness of her love swelled up in my chest, and I erupted in frustration while we were still standing at the door.

"Why did you not call me??? My husband died! It's been eight months! Your daughter is a widow. She is dying, and you feel nothing!" I screamed.

She fired back in retaliation almost instantly, as if she was anticipating this explosion and was prepared to defend herself, "I am also a widow, so what! I have gone through it too! You are no one special!"

I was taken aback.

This pronouncement spiralled into one of her typical meltdowns, the contents of which are usually unrelated to the current topic of discussion. She continued in the same breath, "You don't know what my life has been like. Your brother is always so mean to me; you don't know how he talks to me sometimes. Your nani, she thinks she knows better. She still scolds me like I am a 15-year-old. The help at our house also gives me attitude, like I am a nobody. Your father was a terrible man; he made my life hell!"

This was nothing out of the ordinary; these were the exact hysterical outbursts that I had been witnessing for years now. I knew I didn't have to respond, or even attempt to reason with her, because she wasn't in the present with me anymore; she had teleported to somewhere in her past. None of her rants are ever in the form of coherent, sequential events. They are typically disparate sets of incidents from different pockets of her life, that her mind sews up together in the instant.

Under any other circumstance, I would have chosen to ignore her. I would have walked away while she was still yelling. I wasn't typically crazy enough to engage with her.

But on that day, her outburst enraged me like never before. How dare she! How dare she still think that her trauma was bigger than mine! How dare she think that she still has it worse! I cut her off mid-sentence, shouting at her with the same ferocity, "You are still stuck at what happened twenty years ago! Most of the people you are talking about are dead! You don't even care that your own child is in so much pain!!!"

In response, she screamed even louder. We were in a frenzy—two psychotic women gone berserk, seething with anger at their own broken lives; unleashing their fury at each other, mirroring each other's insanity so flawlessly as only a daughter and mother could.

We continued for a solid twenty minutes before my brother intervened, breaking the stand-off and escorting my mother to the guest bedroom.

I stormed off to my own room and wept into my hands. I wept because, once again, I had been foolish enough to expect something from my mother; and once again, my mother had ruthlessly let me down.

More importantly, I wept because, in that moment of lunacy, I was struck by a terrifying realisation. In a cruel twist of fate, I had somehow ended up becoming what I had tried escaping all my life. In my mother's insanity, I saw mine.

I was slowly *becoming* her—the woman who had lost all sense of her present and had been living, despairing in her past. I realised how my own outbursts were disturbingly similar to hers, explosions of unrelenting rage towards no one in particular but everyone in general. It hit me like a bolt of lightning—I was becoming my mother.

I couldn't fathom how I had ended up here—becoming partly like my mother, furious at the past; partly like my father, pessimistic of the future. My entire life had been a relentless battle to escape my origins, my reality, my past, my parents. But in that moment, it became abundantly clear how miserably and absolutely I had failed at it. I was, alas, the product of those two; the sum of their identities ran alongside the blood flowing in my body. The impression of their lives was so irreversibly etched into my DNA, that even after all these years away from them, it remained stubbornly resolute; leaving me bereft of the freedom from them that I so desperately sought.

That day, coming face to face with my mother's reality terrified me about my own. I couldn't become her; I couldn't live whatever little remained of my life, in misery, like her.

The truth was that there was no one coming to rescue me should I go mad. Sure, Mom and Papa were concerned about my well-being, but they had their own lives and their own grief to deal with. They couldn't possibly have the strength to restrain a third person who was well on the path of self-destruction.

No one was coming. No one had come to pick me up after my father's death. I had had to do it all on my own back then, and I realised that I had to do it on my own *now*.

I reflected on how pathetic I had become, how absorbed I was in my victimhood and misery. How tirelessly I was trying to prove to everyone how tragic my life was, even when no one really seemed to care or fully understand.

Of course, Abhinav was dead; that was a truth no one could deny. But had I genuinely been grieving his death after those first few months? My current discomfort and agony mainly stemmed from the fact that *I* was lost without him. The fifty-year-long life plan that I had in place with him had been shattered into countless little fragments, and in its stead I saw nothing, no hope for my future whatsoever.

It was this that had become the true source of my anguish. My husband was no longer the object of my grief; I had made myself and my life the garish centrepiece of my loss.

30

"Get Back to Life.xlsx" Plan

Consumed by panic, I started grabbing onto anything that I thought could save me. I resolved to fight back my destiny once more, perhaps for one last time.

I started with what was easily accessible and easily digestible. I devoured countless self-improvement videos from popular YouTubers. I picked up several bestselling self-help books and listened to hours and hours of podcasts.

Browsing through the mostly inane videos and books, I stumbled upon an unrelated but intriguing phenomenon. At several places, I found this not-so-subtle glorification of trauma and suffering that left me puzzled. Self appointed self-development gurus applauded stories of present-day heroes—sportspersons, businessmen, internet celebrities—who had suffered abusive childhoods riddled with neglect and, later, a lonely adulthood marred by emotional handicap. But with their unwavering dedication and hard work, the same people had flourished and achieved remarkable success in their respective fields.

The gurus used these examples to illustrate how suffering was what heroes were made of—that with great suffering came great strength of character, that all suffering was, in fact, a catalyst for success.

This discourse was interesting, but seemed heavily biased. While it boasted of the yields of suffering, it seldom delved into the cost of the success that ensued. The ones who suffer and succeed, do they ever feel adequately compensated for their suffering? Was the absolute loss of peace the real reason that those heroes kept pushing? Was the real cost of becoming a hero, the unflinching pain that came before it? These were the questions that continued to bother me, and none of the self-help gurus seemed to address them.

But, I had already paid that cost, I had already lost my peace. Basic human survival was not an option anymore; my suffering had to be transformational.

I first came across the term "post-traumatic growth" in the book *Option B* by Sheryl Sandberg. Post-traumatic growth is essentially a positive psychological change experienced as a result of struggling with highly challenging life circumstances. It is the growth of self and a renewed perspective on the world in the aftermath of trauma.

In my case, what I experienced could be better described as "post-traumatic growth anxiety." The pressure I took on myself was enormous. My life, I began to believe, had to follow the trajectory of a hero of a blockbuster action movie. I was Rocky, the Karate Kid—the underdog.

My destiny had played the first half of the act for me, the act where the hero is crushed beyond recovery. The act where he lies on the ground, breathing heavily, eyes swollen and bloodied, pain consuming every cell of his body. The act where the audience watches him in rapt attention, but none of them expect him to rise.

Then, suddenly, to everyone's disbelief, he stands up, staggering but determined. The crowd first gasps in astonishment and then bursts into thunderous applause.

It was my turn, now, to write the second act, the act where I emerge triumphant despite everything. The act where I stand in a boxing ring as the referee raises my arm above my head. The act where the world gathers around me, awestruck with adulation. The act where my heart swells with jubilation and a wide grin lights up my broken, bloodied face.

But that jubilation and the grin lasts only for a fleeting moment.

Because soon after, I break down into tears. Because it is still not enough. It is still not compensation enough for all that happened—with my father, my mother, Abhinav and me. Nothing will ever be enough.

Yet, basic human survival was not an option anymore.

This treacherous feeling was not new to me. I had learned to thrive on trauma in the past as well. However, with Abhinav's death, the post-traumatic growth anxiety seized me even worse. I spent sleepless, anxious nights sitting on the edge of my bed, lost in deep contemplation. This is a tragedy greater than all the past ones, I'd tell myself, so this time around, I have to strive even harder.

But before I did that, I felt it was necessary to find deliberate, insidious ways to perpetuate my agony as long as I possibly could. Because it was this ruthless agony that was going to shape me into the hero that would justify all this suffering.

I thought of how every single time in the past, I had eventually settled into a fairly stable state, regardless of the size of the tragedies I had survived. The normal amount of anger, the normal amount of anxiousness, the normal amount of otherness from humankind; after the heightened emotions of the initial months of loss. The traumatic events had almost always been fogged out by the humdrum of the present, albeit marked with scattered flashbacks and the occasional nightmare.

But I couldn't let that happen anymore. I couldn't let myself return to a steady state anymore. If this wouldn't change me drastically and irrevocably, nothing else would.

I started out by placing a print-out of Abhinav's photo, the one from the hospital in his purple gown, on the side table of our bed. Underneath it, I wrote in capital letters, "ABHINAV DIED AT 33. YOU COULDN'T SAVE HIM!" Even in the middle of all that madness and chaos, I could recognize how ludicrously toxic this move was, but I felt absolutely compelled to do it.

I placed it there because I needed to look at it first thing in the morning, to remind me of everything that had happened. I placed it there because I wanted Abhinav's death to keep agonising me with the same intensity—five, ten, twenty years down the line. I didn't wish to find peace anymore. I wanted my heart to endlessly burn with the same fire and restlessness as it did during those days.

Then, one Friday night, I settled into my study after wrapping up work and began charting out my *rise from the ashes* story on a Microsoft Excel spreadsheet. I saved the file as "Get Back to Life.xlsx" on my desktop. I sat there for four hours—meticulously crafting a detailed timeline, formatted with coloured rows, milestones and status tracking like the true consultant that I am. The plan was a roadmap for 2022, beginning eight months after my husband's death.

To begin with, I rationed myself another month to cry it all out and simply focus on surviving. After that allocation, I turned my focus to what had been bothering me the most, which was the marked deterioration in my physical appearance: the weight gain, the undereye bags, the acne on my face. I mapped out a row for "Physical Transformation." Starting month nine, I decided to commit myself to rigorous exercising. I planned to join a gym and hire a personal trainer so that by the end of year one, I would reclaim my former self and show the world how it is done.

By the end of the year, I also planned to revamp my wardrobe into a more mature look, that of a no-nonsense middle-aged single woman. I envisioned myself wearing a lot of browns, blacks and other muted pantsuits.

I then mapped a switch from my job to a more challenging role at month fourteen.

I also allocated blocks of time for travel. Travel was essential, for it would serve two purposes: One, escaping the mundanity and reality of my life; Two, finding meaning while meandering through the lanes of a foreign land, much like some of my favourite female authors.

I finally shut my laptop down at 4 am, my colourful spreadsheet looking promising. I was determined. If I can somehow accomplish everything I have jotted down, then voilà, I should be back on my feet in no time.

Little did I know that my grief was a petulant little child who would not conform to my diktats and timelines. I was frustrated when I found myself crying during a client presentation while working from home at month nine. My frustration knew no bounds when I was still struggling to get out of bed on some days, even after almost a year.

I was unable to tame my grief in the way I had anticipated. I didn't shed the weight that I thought I would. Going to the gym felt Herculean, and revamping my wardrobe wasn't the exciting endeavour I thought it would be.

Travelling was the only item on my plan that I was able to strike off, to some extent. Inspired by Abhinav, most of my travels in the initial months were to the mountains in northern India. In the lap of nature, I found a modicum of peace for the first time in several months. My heart ceased its relentless race, even if it was for a fleeting moment. Amidst the mountains and among strangers, I no longer felt like I was lagging behind. I didn't feel like a failure anymore, I was exactly where and what I needed to be.

But once back in my empty home, I would be greeted by my inner demons again. Intense, debilitating anxiety would creep up on me if I would find myself having a normal, relaxing day.

All I had succeeded in accomplishing so far was perpetuating my agony. Each day, I would wake up, gaze at Abhinav's picture by my bedside, and weep for hours together, as my mind would be flooded by flashbacks of those treacherous fifteen days.

I continued to listen to podcasts about productivity hacks. I continued to read self-help books, striving to become the best version of myself. Every few weeks, I would pick a hack, work on it religiously, only to abandon it in frustration because nothing seemed to be changing.

I was growing increasingly impatient with my desire to get better, to get over all of it, to emerge a hero out of it ASAP. It was ironic that while I resented everyone who wanted me to "move on" or who asked me "how long will you brood over it," here I was, unwittingly but tenaciously imposing the same expectations on myself. The urge to come out stronger and mightier, quickly, had possessed me.

***

All over the news, there were reports of new mutations of the virus of varied levels of transmissibility that were being detected every few months.

Around month nine after Abhinav's death, in February 2022, India started witnessing a significant uptick in the number of infected cases once again; the third wave of COVID-19 had arrived, driven by a coronavirus mutation called Omicron. Daily infection numbers began to reach hundreds of thousands once again. My terror-stricken mind began to anticipate the next death in my family—will it be my brother, will it be someone else or will it be me? I desperately wanted it to be me.

Every day, I would wake up and immediately proceed to Google the numbers of new daily COVID-19 cases in India, then in Delhi, then in Jammu, then in Gurgaon, and then I would toggle to the Google Statistics page to look for the number of COVID-19 casualties in each of those areas. This time around, the mortality rates came out to be much lower; the new variants were not as deadly as the Delta variant, which had claimed Abhinav's life. Additionally, a large portion of the country's population was now vaccinated, which also helped.

While I continued to writhe in pain, it seemed like the world was finally on its way to being "normal" again for everyone else.

31

Incurable

I soon reached a point where I knew that I couldn't do it by myself: I needed professional help and I needed it soon.

I began my search for a therapist. I sought out professionals with expertise in PTSD and trauma-informed therapy, terms that I had recently become acquainted with. I found a few who seemed to have decent credentials and good following on Instagram. But I couldn't get any appointments with them; they were all booked solid for a month or more. Therapy and counselling had skyrocketed in demand due to COVID-19.

I didn't have that kind of time. I could see myself edging closer to the threshold of sanity, ready to fall into absolute lunacy any second.

Finally, after a week of research, I zeroed down on one therapist. She was a woman, around the same age as me. She seemed well qualified based on her degrees listed on LinkedIn and came across as kind and approachable, so I decided to take a leap of faith and booked an online session with her.

At the beginning of my first session, as I sat awkwardly in front of my laptop with my camera on, she asked me after the initial pleasantries, "What brings you here?"

I had shared with her a brief account of my life in a call before the session, so I was initially puzzled when she posed this question. But then, she insisted that I talk about those experiences in more detail.

Almost instantly, I let out a tsunami of words in broken sentences. "My father died…I saw him die in front of my eyes…then, my uncles died…we all lived in the same house…I saw so many dead people…then, my husband died a few months ago. I saw him die, too…my mom is mentally ill…I have no one. I don't think I am going to survive this. There is no way out for me." I burst into tears as I tried to summarise decades of trauma in one breath.

In a way, it was liberating to unleash all my pent-up emotions in front of a stranger without the fear of judgement, without feeling that I was bothering them with my life's misery (given that I was paying them to listen to me), without the worry of being perceived as weak, without having to hear the response, "It's not all that bad, at least you have a job."

It was a relief to finally find a release for the world that had been building inside me block by block for months now. It was a relief to be able to assign words and sentences to my trauma. It was a relief to be able to piece together the sequence of events that had led me to this very point in life.

I noticed her diligently taking notes, which seemed promising. I was overly optimistic as I wiped my tears.

The first few questions I asked her when I finally caught my breath were, "Am I scarred for life? Will this completely destroy me mentally and physically? Will I become like my mother? Will I ever be able to live a normal life?"

She responded with a calm, straight face, "Well, the fact that you are thinking about it and the fact that you are here to seek help means something. It is, if nothing else, a step in the right direction."

The subsequent sessions continued similarly, with me rambling about my misery, my fears, how broken I was and how unempathetic the world seemed. To each outburst, she would mostly pose the same question, "And how do you feel about it?" I would respond with more misery and more anger, which she would follow up with another, "And how does that make you feel?" And I would go on again.

Initially, I had so much to unload that the whole process felt cathartic. But after a certain point, it felt like our conversations were going in circles. It was a narrative of misery begetting more misery.

I started getting impatient. "When are we getting to the solving part of it?" I wanted to ask. I felt the growing need to interrupt her and to shift the focus of our discussion to making it more solution-oriented, "But how can I get better? How can I end this cycle of misery?" With all the details that I had shared with her so far, I had hoped that she would be able to offer me a "quick fix" to accelerate my recovery.

Subconsciously, I was hoping for her to give me an antidote that would make it all go away, that would at least make it all bearable. If not that, I was hopeful she would utilise the theories and methods that she must have learned in her psychology class to: stop me from going insane, to fog the nightmares that I had every night, to block the constant cacophony of voices in my head and the relentless drowning feeling in my chest.

She was a professional after all; she should be able to fix me; she should have a textbook solution to my situation.

However, to my dismay, all I got was, "Your grief will not diminish; you will simply learn to grow around it as you create more life experiences and form new relationships." This was not new information to me; I was already aware of it. Almost all the articles about grief and healing I had read reiterated this concept. They all had this one graphic with a series of pictures. There is a jar (your life) and a stone (your grief). In picture number one, the "grief stone" occupies the entirety of the "life jar," leaving no room for anything else. However, in the following pictures, while the "grief stone" retains its size, the "life jar" expands to make space for other experiences.

It was all logical, but it wasn't enough to save my sinking soul. It was not the magic wand that I was seeking. So I decided to move on to another therapist, hoping she would know better.

And then the next.

None of it worked; I was writing them off one after the other.

It was because even before meeting with the first therapist, I had completed my own diagnosis and concluded that my trauma was incurable. I was convinced that I would, inevitably, go insane. How could I not go insane? It was unfair to demand any sanity from me.

I believed that even the best therapists in the country couldn't help me. My trauma was so unique and so life-shattering that none of them could possibly understand, let alone provide a solution. I was arrogant in the assessment of my condition; to me my infliction felt absolutely unique, and the anguish that it caused felt even more unique.

I had deemed myself unsavable.

Part VI

Living Without Them

32

The Love of Romantic Novels

As a young adult growing up in a family with mostly dysfunctional relationships, my expectation of love fluctuated between two extremes.

On most days, I accepted that I might never have a stable relationship with another human being. I resigned myself to the belief that I was incapable of both loving and being loved, that "love" was a feeling reserved for others. The idea of being in a romantic relationship, let alone getting married, felt beyond my reach.

Yet, on rare, exceptionally optimistic days, I would secretly hope that a handsome knight in shining armour would show up at my doorstep one day to rescue me from all my misery and whisk me away to a world of perpetual happiness. I would miraculously shed all that I was; to become something new, something beautiful, something worthy of someone's love.

Three years into my father's death, things were beginning to stabilise. I had successfully completed my business programme and secured a decent job with a consulting firm in Gurgaon. Meanwhile, my brother, who had been battling his own demons, had also begun to find some stability in his life. The family disputes that had erupted following the deaths of my father and uncles were slowly subsiding as well.

I saw it all as a glimmer of hope and I grabbed it with both my hands. Maybe I too had a shot. Maybe I can still make a normal life for myself.

When I first began talking to Abhinav, I was posted on a work assignment in the US while he was in Delhi. I was supposed to be gone for three months, so technically we had to wait for that much time before we could finally meet in person.

I saw this period as the perfect test. If we could manage to survive the three months without meeting, there was certainly some compatibility between the two of us.

With Abhinav, I felt a unique sense of familiarity that you don't often feel with a stranger—when there is something about them that makes you think that you know them from before, but you can't quite pinpoint from where. He was incredibly easy to talk to, and as an introvert, it was such a relief—conversations flowed effortlessly.

During the initial days, we had a perfect routine in place. He would call me almost every evening, right at the end of my day, once he had reached his office and after he had tackled his tasks for the morning. The timing worked well for both of us, despite being in time zones that were ten hours apart.

Often during our conversations, if he veered to a topic in which I showed little interest, like "waxing the oranges" (he was working in an agri products supply chain company at the time and talked a lot about fruits and cold storage), he would swiftly switch the subject. In an attempt to regain my attention, he would transition to something lighter, like Page 3 gossip, "Did you hear that so-and-so actors are having an affair?" He would name such an unlikely pair that I would burst into uncontrollable laughter. "Come on! Is that really true? I don't believe you. What's the source of this information?"

To which he would respond slyly, "It's all top secret and classified, I can't reveal it to you."

I would text him throughout my day, even when I knew he would be fast asleep. I'd send him pictures of the many misspelt versions of my name that the Starbucks baristas would scribble on my takeaway cups. I would send him voice notes describing events from the day that I couldn't wait to tell him about. I would send him long videos capturing the first snowfall of the season and snapshots of the beautiful graffiti that I would stumble upon on the way back from work.

He had already become "my person."

I was returning to India for the fourth death anniversary of my dad. It is a huge milestone in Hindu customs, known as the chaubarsi, which involves a grand feast for all the deceased's relatives. My father's chaubarsi was falling somewhere in late April, as per the Hindu calendar. My plan was to first visit Jammu to be with my family, then head to Delhi to meet Abhinav.

At home, things had started looking up. My brother appeared cheerful for the first time in years. All the cousins had gathered together after a long time. We talked, we laughed, we celebrated the fact that we had survived.

It could only get better from here.

Though May is unarguably the most tragic month of the year for me now, it is also the month that had once brought with it the exhilaration of new love. It was the month that I first met Abhinav.

We met at a restaurant that he had picked, a fancy Indian fusion food place. I gave him full points for that. I dressed up in a cute black skirt and a striped tee, an outfit to subtly signal "cute but not trying too hard" and arrived fifteen minutes before our agreed-upon time. Abhinav, however, showed up twenty minutes late. In fact, if I remember clearly, he was late to almost all our first few dates. Punctuality was important to me, so I deducted a few points for that.

I watched him as he walked towards me. Standing at almost 5'9", he seemed slightly shorter than I had pictured him. Of course, this is coming from someone who is barely 5'1". But hey, a woman can dream!

Despite the scorching Delhi summer, he arrived wearing a casual cream blazer over a blue buttoned shirt adorned with small white motifs. The sweltering heat, with temperatures exceeding forty degree Celsius, had him perspiring visibly.

He apologised profusely as he wiped the sweat off his face with his handkerchief, "Sorry for keeping you waiting, I had a meeting with some distributors and I am coming directly from there." We ordered something to drink as he settled in.

I was a bit flustered and found it challenging to look him in the eye initially; first meetings aren't really my strong suit. But as soon as he launched into his trademark jokes and his insider Bollywood news, I couldn't help but break into a wide grin. The familiarity that was hazy at the start slowly came back to me with each passing minute. It turned out to be the most successful first date I had ever been to.

For our second date, to my utter astonishment, he took me to an all-you-can-eat Sunday brunch. He even advised me to skip breakfast that morning to ensure we got our money's worth. To top it off, he brought a bouquet of lilies to what appeared to be a mukbang date. As I started making faces after a few servings, because I was already stuffed, he jokingly quipped, "You are a disgrace to buffets. Restaurants make a ton of money from buffets because of people like you. I am not taking you to another one ever again." We laughed about it all day.

I don't know after how many such dates, but I had started falling for this ever-grinning boy from Delhi who insisted that I should address him not as my "boy-friend" but my "man-friend," his rationale being that he had just turned thirty.

With no real life precedents to draw from, my definition of love was shaped by what I had seen in the movies or read in romance novels. It was the hero frantically rushing to stop the heroine from boarding her flight, emotively professing his love for her, declaring that he couldn't bear to let go of her, that it would shatter his world and ruin his life if they didn't end up together.

It was the elusive "spark" that two strangers shared when their eyes met across the room. It was the constant butterflies in the gut and the ceaseless longing to find safety in the arms of the one you loved and desired. It was the burning passion of the hearts and the bodies, so intense that it could possibly destroy you.

My story with Abhinav, to some extent, did manage to live up to the hype of the world of romantic fantasies.

It was July 2019, and we had been dating for a while. I was stationed in Boston for a project and Abhinav decided to come visit me for a few days. Thrilled beyond words, I wanted to take him everywhere—my office in the City Center, my favourite coffee spots on Newbury Street, trip to Cape Cod and the lively lanes of Quincy Market.

In the weeks leading up to his arrival, my weekends were dedicated to putting together a meticulously planned day-to-day itinerary.

Along with spending time in Boston, we also decided to make a pit stop in Chicago to meet some of Abhinav's friends. Since his visit coincided with the

4th of July week, we planned to watch the customary fireworks at the Chicago Navy Pier.

On that day, we chose to spend most of our time in the hotel, as the city was expected to be packed with crowds. It wasn't until evening that we ventured out. The streets were bustling even more than we had anticipated. As we approached the pier, we noticed that people had been up there for hours and had already occupied the good viewing spots.

Having experienced enough firework displays during Diwali celebrations and Delhi weddings, I wasn't too fixated on a perfect view. We managed to find a decent spot on the rooftop of a building and patiently waited for the show to begin. The fireworks display started at 9 pm and illuminated the night sky for around twenty minutes.

Once the show concluded, the crowd started to drift towards the exit of the pier, and so did we.

Suddenly, we sensed a commotion in the crowd. We could hear people at a distance shouting, "Gunshots!" "Someone has been shot!" "Take cover!" A sudden hysteria ensued. The visuals of recent gun violence incidents in the US flashed across my mind and I began to panic.

Since the supposed gunshots had been heard outside the pier, the crowd began to hastily retreat back into the pier.

It all unfolded so quickly that I couldn't process or comprehend what was happening. I just held on to Abhinav's hand tightly while he tried to navigate us through the frantic crowd. He appeared to be much calmer and in control than I was in that bewildering moment.

And then, I saw swarms of frenzied people running towards us. I froze in fear. The scene quickly escalated into a chaotic stampede with us in the middle of it. As I stumbled and fell, a few people stepped over me. I gave out a desperate screech "Abhinavvvvv", as I began to feel choked. I kept clinging to his hand as he held on to mine, but our grip had begun to weaken and our hands had slowly started slipping away from each other.

Abhinav acted quickly; he pulled me up with a sudden jerk and guided us through the mob to a safe spot behind a nearby building. My legs were covered in painful bruises that had blood oozing out of them, and I was beginning to limp.

We stood there hiding and waiting for the situation to calm down, gripped by fear for our lives and our minds fogged with confusion. Abhinav looked at my terrified face, smiled and remarked, "At least we got the full Chicago experience."

The chaos persisted for some time. Beside us, a distraught woman wailed loudly and repeatedly called out, "Ashley! Ashleyyyy!!! I am here!" The sound of sirens from police vans and ambulances filled the air. There were pieces of broken glass from shattered windows and abandoned footwear scattered all across the streets.

My heart continued to thump loudly.

Soon enough, it became apparent that it was a false alarm. There was no crazy gunman on the loose. A brawl had erupted among local gangs outside the pier and someone had stabbed a member of the other gang. Two of them were badly injured, but there were no gunshots.

The whole ordeal lasted for close to an hour. Subsequently, the police began clearing the area and we managed to find our way back to the hotel. I was traumatised, but also glad that we were both safe.

Back at the hotel, Abhinav managed to arrange for some dressing material for my wounds. As I settled on the sofa, he positioned himself on the carpet beside me with his legs crossed and gently tended to my injuries. I looked at him as he carefully applied the dressing on my wounds. I would have been trampled to death if he wasn't there. He had saved me.

It was a perfect, magical moment straight out of the movies, with the man I had fallen deeply in love with by my side. And in that moment, he was my hero, my knight in shining armour who had come to salvage me from the ruins of my life.

Without giving it much thought, I blurted out, "Well, while you are down there, you might as well propose to me." He turned his handsome face up to look me in the eye, smiled and took my hand to say, "Ms. Senior Consultant, will you do me the honour of marrying me?"

33

The Boring Kind of Love

Of all the adventures that we end up going on with someone, it is almost always the boring ones that we miss them for.

Most of my courtship with Abhinav had to be done long distance; we would meet after months at a stretch. The time we did get together, we would spend travelling and going on fancy dates; the thrill and excitement of new love at every reunion still intact. It was surreal and romantic—just like I had always imagined it to be.

Which is why when we got married and were locked down 24x7 because of the pandemic, I was gripped by a sudden, almost irrational fear—that we were doomed. We were bound to fall apart, and quickly. I loved Abhinav and he loved me, but I was also acutely aware that we were two very different people.

Abhinav was outgoing, relatively calm and fairly social, while I was his diametric opposite. I feared that without the usual external stimuli of travelling, eating out and socialising with friends, we might not have a lot to salvage our relationship, from the inherent conflict of our vastly different personalities. I knew that, sooner or later, I will have one of my depressive episodes and Abhinav will not be able to weather through it. He will, inevitably, wake up one day to the real me and not find me or my quirks loveable anymore.

I knew that all of this was bound to happen—even without the pandemic and the lockdown—but I had hoped that the revelation would be gradual, with our other commitments coming in our way of unravelling each other.

A couple of weeks into the lockdown, however, I began to realise how all my fears were unfounded. There was no clash between our personalities, no portentous disagreements. Instead, I ended up falling for Abhinav even more, and in the process, ended up discovering an entirely new kind of love that was completely foreign to me until then.

It wasn't the kind of love that you typically saw in the movies, and yet it truly swept me off my feet. It was not the kind of love that made your heart skip a beat; instead it slowed your heartbeat down to a steady rhythm that you wish you'd never escape. It was the kind of love that may seem ordinary and mundane on the face of it but was spectacularly exhilarating when you looked close enough.

It was love that I didn't even know existed, but from the moment I stumbled upon it, I knew it was all that I ever wanted.

It was the wondrous feeling of slow, lazy weekend mornings, of binge-watching TV shows cuddled on cold winter nights, of giving each other hot oil champis, of experimenting new recipes together, of late-night conversations in bed in hushed voices, even when we were the only souls in the entire house. I had fallen deeply in love with how our lives and identities—inherently so divergent—were beautifully coming together in the rented apartment that we'd made our home.

All my life, I had believed that I wouldn't know how to love, because my parents didn't teach me, because my life didn't let me, because of who I essentially was: inherently unlovable. But love, perhaps, doesn't need to be taught. Even if you haven't ever seen it before, even if you haven't felt it before, you would still, invariably, know how to love. Because it is love that is the most intrinsic of all human reflexes; because it is love that comes most effortlessly to each one of us.

Soon, I didn't have to pretend to be someone else with Abhinav. I could be who I was—and it was such a relief. He now knew all my triggers and would dash to stroke my hair on finding me curled into a ball of anxiety in bed. He would find me in my worst pyjamas and still say, "You look nice." On one occasion, I burnt a significant portion of my hair trying a new hair treatment. I looked horrendous. When I returned home in tears and showed Abhinav the disaster, he casually remarked, "It's nothing, looks fine to me. If you want, we can get you a wig. But it has to be an interesting colour, maybe blue or burgundy."

While he did do all of that, he was still far from the "rom com" romantic I wished him to be. To nudge him to articulate his feelings for me more extravagantly, I would sometimes playfully quiz him. "Give me ten reasons why you love me. You have until the end of the day."

He would look at me puzzled, and then would spend the entire day coming up with an answer that would appease me.

He would begin with something like, "You are smart, you are stunning." When that would not satisfy me, he would attempt some more, "You are adorable, you are witty." I would still not be pleased. "Those are such generic traits. Anyone could be smart, funny, beautiful. What is it specifically about *me* that makes you love me?" He would try hard all day, but just to mess with him I would keep shooting all his answers down.

Then, the very next day, I would find a bouquet of roses, exactly ten fragrant blooms, placed on our living room coffee table. He wouldn't say a word about them, and I would know that I didn't need those ten reasons after all.

34

Move On

In the fifteen tumultuous days that we spent in the hospital, there were fleeting moments filled with the pure warmth of togetherness that kept us going despite all the torment and loss of hope.

I remember this one occasion when Abhinav was sitting on his bed, immersed deep in contemplation. To distract him from what I presumed were negative thoughts about his deteriorating health, I touched his hand and asked, "What's going on?"

Perhaps to diffuse the situation, he quipped "You are taking such good care of me. See, I have finally domesticated you," and gave me a goofy wink. I playfully pursed my lips and widened my eyes, pretending to be offended. He knew that as a modern independent woman, I hated that word and what it implied.

He then paused for a couple of seconds, his facial expressions slightly intensified, "Don't you worry, I will get better soon. And when we are pregnant, I will take good care of you, just as you have been taking care of me."

It wasn't entirely unexpected—we had recently begun thinking about starting a family and had been discussing timelines for parenthood. I looked into his eyes, his hands tightly clasped into mine, "You will be the best father in the whole world."

How do I move on from that? To all the people who casually walked up to me and asked me to simply "move on"—my friends, family, random strangers I've met along the way—I genuinely ask: how *do* I move on? How do I tame the whirlwind of emotions that surges in my heart every time I reflect on that moment, brimming with so much promise and hope? How do I move on from the man who, at the most precarious time of his life, saw me as the mother of his child? Where do I even begin?

As part of my "get back to life" plan, I did give serious thought to the idea of finding a partner again. I had all this newfound love that Abhinav had seeded in my heart and sprouted with his warmth; which now sat heavy on my chest, puzzled, trying to find him, trying to find the familiar feeling that it had grown so accustomed to, that had so suddenly abandoned it. Where was all this love supposed to go, now that he wasn't there anymore?

But how do I move on when the baggage feels so exhausting and closure so improbable?

Of course, I know people who have lost their spouses and found love again, but I always wonder how difficult it must be for them—not having completely stopped loving someone, but having to open their hearts to the possibility of falling in love with someone new. How excruciating it must be to find that delicate balance of not letting go of the past that they shared with their late partners while trying to build a future with someone new.

I wonder what happens to the million little things that they have of their late partners—pictures, clothes, shoes, letters. Do they discard them or do they keep those mementoes tucked away in a box of memories, hidden from plain sight, as if out of guilt?

I wonder if there are things and feelings and people and places that remind them of their lost love—but do they bury those thoughts deep in their hearts, fearing hurting their new partners?

I wonder if the new partners are riddled with the feeling of unrelinquished love—that they would perhaps never be loved with the same ferocity as their partners' deceased loves, that death had perhaps strengthened their bond like nothing else ever could?

What a struggle it must be to keep such a relationship going.

How can I possibly move on when the *idea* of the relationship that I had with Abhinav becomes more and more perfect with each passing day? It's as if we were *always* truly, madly and deeply in love. It's as if we were inseparable. It's as if we never really had any differences.

But we certainly did have our differences. I recall Abhinav and I engaging in heated arguments over trivial matters. I remember occasionally nagging him about certain habits of his that I didn't particularly like. But after he died, it's as if those conflicts ceased to exist and Abhinav became blameless, without fault.

Death has fogged my memory of all his inadequacies and all the incompatibilities of our relationship.

It's possible that I am more in love with the *idea* of him today than I was in love with him when he was alive. Perhaps if we had lived our story to its natural end, running into decades of history together, our relationship would have turned out to be as ordinary as others: two mundane lives, riddled with regular conflict, punctuated by fleeting moments of togetherness.

Maybe our story is so brilliantly perfect in my mind because, like all timeless love stories, it remains unfinished, marked by our separation. We could have been anything together—I could make it anything I wish it to be. How could anyone ever compete with such a perfect ghost?

***

How do I move on to someone else when I am convinced that I will bring death upon them as well?

When Abhinav and I started getting serious about our relationship, I often wondered if I truly deserved this future with him, given the past that I had lived through. But as our relationship progressed seamlessly, my fears began to assuage. Still, my past would creep up on me from time to time, making me anxious about the future. I tried hard to reason with my fears—Abhinav has fairly healthy habits, his parents don't have any major health problems, he doesn't stress easily. Nothing untoward should happen to him.

As the days, months and years passed, I became less vigilant. And that's when life caught me off guard.

I could have denied it when Dad died; I could have still denied it when my uncles died; but how could I deny it anymore? The three decades of misfortune that I had brought upon the people around me confirmed only one thing: that I was inexorably cursed.

So, if by some twist of fate, I did happen to find another man in the future, and by some stroke of luck we do end up together, I am convinced that something tragic would happen to him as well. An untimely death has started to seem like an unavoidable culmination of every relationship I enter.

And soon enough, everyone will know.

Something that was my dark little secret, something that people might have talked about in hushed voices but never out in the open, that something would become common knowledge among all—I was the one and only source of all the tragedy around.

I dread that the world would call me a witch and hand me the punishment that deep down I know I truly deserve. They would tie me up and set me ablaze, watch me burn to ashes in the relief that I couldn't kill anymore. I would burn in the flames that should have engulfed me long ago, before I could have caused all the devastation that I did.

I couldn't let that happen; I couldn't let the truth play itself out.

35

Absolutely, Completely Free

I was first introduced to Mrs. Sachdeva through a Facebook group for widows affected by COVID-19. The group brought together women from various backgrounds, ages and parts of the country, all bound by the same loss.

She appeared to be in her early fifties and had been invited by our group to deliver a session on Zoom, where she generously shared her experience of coping with grief in the aftermath of her husband's death. Her husband had succumbed to cancer of the bone marrow a few years back. Serene and composed, she spoke eloquently about her journey after her loss, talking about acceptance and growth and moments that changed her perspective on life in recent years.

I felt immediately drawn to her tranquil demeanour. As I absorbed her words, I wished I could be like her someday—to talk with the same clarity, thoughtfulness and reflection about the traumatic events of my life. I wished that one day I, too, could have the courage to recount my story like she did—without getting agitated as the words poured out of my mouth, without tears welling up in my eyes, without a storm of fury rising in my chest.

I began to believe that she was the one who held the key to all my questions, that she was the one who could save me. I found myself desperate to connect with her; desperate for her reassurance that I could weather this storm, that I could survive it as well, just as she had.

I looked her up on LinkedIn, where she was listed as a Life Coach. Initially, I was sceptical of the qualifications and skills associated with the title, but I couldn't help myself; I had to speak with her. I messaged her and arranged to connect online on Sunday mornings.

Our first few sessions followed a similar routine to the consultations I had had with therapists. Under the weight of my grief, I would simply crumble in front of her. But unlike the therapists, she wouldn't respond with the nonchalant, "And how does that make you feel?"

Perhaps she knew how it made me feel, because she had felt the exact flurry of emotions herself not so long ago. She smiled, like it all made sense to her, and calmly remarked, "Nobody can truly understand until they live it themselves."

Almost immediately, it was as if a burden had been lifted off my chest. I felt vindicated. My angst and my frustration felt validated. I was not agonising over nothing. I wasn't crazy after all. I saw hope for myself for the very first time in almost a year.

We continued to meet online for an hour on Sunday mornings. She would have questions and exercises ready for me for every session. I would run out of breath every time trying to narrate the events of my life. She would help me calm down with breathing exercises, which, to my surprise, I did find soothing.

With what seemed like genuine interest, she would ask me questions about Abhinav—questions that no therapist had ever brought up, questions that family and friends didn't dare bring up anymore: "What was Abhinav like?" "What do you miss about him the most?" My face would light up as I'd launch into lengthy monologues about all things Abhinav.

But again, after the first few sessions, impatience started to creep in. I wanted the answers to my pain; I wanted the solution right away. I started to bring up my "getting better" questions: "Will this pain ever go away? Will I go insane?"

She sensed my desperation and suggested, "Let's start small. How about you start with a gratitude journal? Every day, for the next few months, why don't you jot down three things you're grateful for? Even when you feel there is nothing left to live for, I am sure there must be a few things in your life that you still appreciate. It can be something small or it can be something big. You can even repeat the same three things on multiple days if you can't find anything new. But you need to do it every day, without fail."

Keeping a gratitude journal didn't seem transformational. It felt like a modest tool to navigate a highly convoluted problem. I had made numerous attempts at maintaining a gratitude journal in the past, but I would always struggle to keep up with the practice. Even if I did manage to stick with it for a while, it never elicited any noticeable change in my outlook towards life.

But my trust in Mrs. Sachdeva ran deep, and I was genuinely open and willing to try her methods and approaches. I couldn't dismiss her like I had dismissed the therapists, because I truly believed that her wisdom stemmed from her very own experience with loss.

So, with a lot of initial reluctance, I agreed to give the gratitude journal another chance. Every evening, after wrapping up my work, I would settle onto my bed and note down three things I was grateful for. Finding things to be grateful for wasn't that challenging. Despite all the tragedy and bouts of self-indulgent misery, there was still plenty worth appreciating in my life. I hadn't entirely lost sight of that. On the very first day, I wrote:

"I am financially stable."

"I am able-bodied and not physically dependent on anyone."

"I have friends and family who still check up on me regularly, even when I haven't been responding to them."

Then I wrote:

"My brother finally has a stable job."

"Papa, Mom tolerate me, despite all the tantrums I have thrown."

"I have support from my work to start slow, and to take time to recover from my loss."

"I visited my favourite coffee shop today."

While I still remained uncertain about the efficacy of gratitude journaling, it did compel me to deliberately think through the aspects of my life which, despite everything, were still working in my favour. Much to my surprise, I found myself not having to repeat the same things that I was grateful for that often.

Then, on one particular evening, with lot of hesitation I wrote—

"I am absolutely, completely free."

—and violently scratched it off immediately, nearly tearing the entire page off. It felt wrong.

It was the silver lining that my self-absorbed mind was nudging me to find in the death of my husband. How atrociously selfish the thought was! How persistent was my soul's hunger for survival that it was willing to see a bright side to the death of the human it deeply cherished! How profoundly the desire to unearth hope had poisoned me!

Thereafter, I stopped keeping the journal altogether. I gave some vague excuses to Mrs. Sachdeva on why I no longer wished to continue the practice and how it was not helping me at all.

But that was the undeniable truth—for the very first time in my life, I was, indeed, absolutely and completely free.

In the three decades of my existence, all I had ever done was what I believed was expected of me. I got myself an engineering degree, spent a couple of years in an IT company, earned another degree and then started working in the corporate world. I had found myself a suitable man and married him. I was tirelessly agreeable at my job, at home and with the rest of the world. I was content at being a shadow, a supporting character in the narrative of everyone else's story, with no desire for anyone's attention and no wish to be the centre of any discourse.

Nobody had coerced me into any of it. It was a series of choices that I had voluntarily made because they appeared to be rational; because everyone around me was making more or less the same choices; leading more or less the same lives. I was a hamster running on my wheel without having made the conscious choice to do so. I was trusting the collective intellect of all the other hamsters to show me the way.

One day, abruptly, my wheel broke down, and with a tremendous jolt, I fell off it and tumbled out of my cage.

I was shocked and distraught. I stood there, disheartened, staring at the other hamsters gleefully running away on their wheels; then at my own wheel, which lay shattered into pieces.

With the trauma and agony that ensued, had also emerged a freedom so absolute that I was, first, unaware of it and, later, unaccepting of it. I was broken, yet I was absolutely free. Nobody really expected anything of me anymore. No more pressure to get married, no longer an expectation to bear children. At work, nobody expected me to out-perform others. I could slag, I could fall behind. No one really expected me to win at anything anymore. I was no longer in the race anymore; the rules did not apply to me anymore

The blend of this absolute freedom mixed with the perils of post traumatic growth anxiety was a potent concoction that I didn't know how to handle. Sitting in my living room, I would think of small changes I could make to my miserable life. "Maybe I should just go for a drastic haircut. Abhinav would have loved that; he loved it when I experimented with my hair."

Other times, I would contemplate making more radical choices, "Should I move to another country and start a new life altogether?" "Should I retire from my job and start freelancing?" "Maybe I need to start a podcast just like Mo Gawdat did after the loss of his son."

I was overwhelmed by the array of options I was suddenly presented with. Up until then, I had been treading the path that everyone else did, but now my story had diverged, and it had diverged so significantly that I couldn't follow their lead anymore. I had to forge my own unique path, and the very thought of it was terrifying.

There were also a slew of entirely new choices and decisions that had popped up after Abhinav's death. A gynaecologist friend suggested I consider freezing my eggs if I ever wanted to have children. I did wish to have children, but that desire was intertwined with Abhinav. How could I ever imagine having children without him?

Papa wanted me to move out of my rented place to a permanent apartment somewhere in Gurgaon. I understood his concerns, but I kept dodging the question. Abhinav and I had made a pact that we would not settle down in one place until we were well into our fifties, and when we eventually did, it would be in a retirement house outside the city. How could I then take this decision alone?

The freedom at my doorstep and the myriad questions and advice from all corners pestered me; they were forcing me to think about my path forward, my story henceforth. They were persistently nudging me to embark on a journey different from the one I had originally set out on with my husband.

My life was frozen in the moment when I was waiting outside the ICU room for Abhinav; and more than a year later, I still stood there, firm, not knowing where to go from there.

36

My Story

Among his other professional experiences, Abhinav's bio on LinkedIn also lists, "World Traveller: August 2014 to April 2015." Having spent just under two years in the corporate world after graduating, Abhinav decided to resign from his fairly well-adjusted job and embark on a backpacking adventure across thirty countries in Europe, Asia, Australia and New Zealand for nine months.

Papa and Mom often recount that time and share stories of their initial less-than-enthusiastic reaction when he first revealed his plans to them. They had attempted to dissuade him, to coax him into taking a sabbatical later on instead, once he was established in his career. But he didn't budge; his mind was made up.

During his MBA, which is typically a fast-paced course with very little time to focus on your personal life let alone go on extended adventures, Abhinav chose to enrol in a 45-day mountaineering course in Manali. While he was savouring his time in the mountains, Papa found himself pleading with the admin office at Abhinav's college to not mark him short in attendance and let him sit for the upcoming exams. Papa loves to narrate this incident again and again, with a broad smile on his face, in a way that only a father does when fondly recalling the past mischiefs of his now-adult son.

Not that Abhinav was entirely reckless as a young man and completely disregarded all rules and regulations. In fact, he did end up successfully completing his MBA with fairly good grades and managed to secure a decent job once back from his travels.

But *this* was what Abhinav was for me. Of whatever I knew of him, he stood as the absolute antithesis of all I had known before him—a resolute, self-assured human who was not a regular hamster like me.

Among the meticulously organised folders in his hard drives, lies a treasure trove of stories from his travels—memories neatly arranged by country, location, year and month of his adventures. Every now and then, I find myself browsing through them in an attempt to get to know my husband a little more.

Within those folders are hundreds of pictures of him, in most of which he appears deeply tanned and noticeably leaner than I remember him to be. He must have been in his early twenties at the time, yet he looks more like a 16-year-old boy. His sun-kissed face is gleaming with his familiar wide smile and squinting eyes. Surrounding him are young men and women of diverse ethnicities and ages, all posing and smiling alongside him.

It is strange how he was touching so many lives in those fleeting moments, as he travelled from one country to another; and how those lives were leaving their imprints on him, shaping him into the man I met and married.

Maybe that is why I was smitten with him from the get go. Perhaps opposites do attract. I could never imagine voluntarily stirring up my life to jump into the kind of uncertainty that he did. I, on the contrary, had always been a sucker for normalcy, for stability. Perhaps the reason that I found myself instantly drawn to him was because I could never be him.

His life and its essence is succinctly summed up in his WhatsApp status, which to date reads "Get Busy Living" accompanied by a series of emoticons: a couple with a heart popping between them, a mountain, a flexed muscle and a plate of food. That was all that mattered to him, and perhaps in that specific order. He sure did live a life that was marked by conscious choices and deliberate decisions.

Sometimes I wish Abhinav had lived much longer than he did, not for my sake or for the sake of Mom and Papa, but for his own sake, for the sake of the incredible life of wonderful choices he would have lived, for the sake of the remarkable story his life would have been.

When I reflect upon Abhinav's story, I am often compelled to consider my own alongside his, and it pales terribly in comparison. While his story is marked by a series of conscious choices to lead his life a certain way, my story, thus far, had been unconsciously unfolding in reaction to everything else around me. It was a story of predestined misery, a story that had sucked every ounce of vitality out of me, sparing nothing for any conscious effort to mould it in any way.

To onlookers, my story might appear to be about an unnatural tryst with death, but for me, it is also about a lifelong yearning for normalcy, a desire to blend in and belong with the rest of them.

For as long as I could remember, I had always felt like an outcast. Like a little child peeping through the glass windows of a shiny toy store, I watched the world from outside. I watched: the carefree laughs, the unhindered familial love, the absence of constant conflict and contempt, the bounty of health and the moderation of disease. On some days, my inner child would be overly optimistic, nurturing the hope that one day she would be invited inside this dreamy store. Yet, on most days, she had learned to be content with being an outsider, an observer—relishing the spectacle but also resigning herself to her fate.

When I was younger, I hoped for my parents to reconcile and be a "normal" couple. In my early twenties, in addition to that, I wanted my father to be of "normal" health. As I entered my late twenties and all hopes for my father ceased with his death, I hoped for my Mom to be "normal" as signs of her mental illness worsened.

Then I met Abhinav, and for the very first time in my life, I was no longer an outcast.

To me, he was the enchanted doorway to the shiny store that I had been standing outside of all this while. The union with him was supposed to be the juncture where my life would begin to merge with the world around me. Regardless of how flawed my past might have been, with Abhinav by my side, I was one of them.

All my life, all I had ever wanted, was normalcy. Yet it was normalcy that had persistently eluded me.

***

In one of my early sessions with Mrs. Sachdeva, when I was still filled with agitation and anger, and I kept rambling on about, "Why does it keep happening to me?" "Why am I being tested again?" She interrupted my sobs and tried to comfort me, "Maybe because you have a special destiny carved out for you." I

188

momentarily stopped wailing and listened to what else she had to say, only that I was not listening anymore.

My mind raced at those words. "Perhaps my life is not normal because it is meant to be special," I told myself. She had probably said that to calm me down, but some part of me deeply, desperately wanted to believe that I was, in fact, special.

It wanted to believe that there was a reason that of all the people that Abhinav could have ended up with, he ended up with me; that it was not all for nothing. It wanted to believe that Abhinav's unbridled spirit had chosen me of all people because it was drawn to something in my spirit which was not chained to the normal, something that matched its own courage and free spiritedness.

To live a story that was worth living, I had to set myself free from the pursuit of "normal," which clearly didn't want me, and start embracing the "abnormal"—the chaos, the fears, the anxieties and the aberrations that made me. I needed to welcome this "abnormal" with open arms and give my old friend a tight hug, for I knew it was here to stay.

37

Meaning of Life

"To live is to suffer, to survive is to find some meaning in the suffering."

– Frederick Nietzsche

Relentless thoughts about life, meaning, suffering and purpose don't plague your mind unless something tremendous happens—something that jolts you to your core and questions the very foundation of your entire existence. But once that something tremendous *does* happen, meaning becomes the all-consuming, continuously looming thought that haunts you night and day.

Unable to get any inspiration from all the content I continued to consume online, my search for answers to my misery, after a long year, pivoted me in an entirely new direction. It all started when I first stumbled upon Maya Angelou's *I Know Why the Caged Bird Sings,* and her story of triumph over a tough childhood riddled with brutal racism and ruthless trauma. My struggles seemed trivial and my life privileged in comparison to hers. But more importantly, her story stirred up something inside my soul that I hadn't felt in a year.

I instantly knew where I needed to look.

I began searching for bestselling memoirs by women, for heartwarming stories about extraordinary women who kept going against all odds. I immersed myself in *The Glass Castle* by Jeannette Walls, her story of growing up with nomadic parents and unwavering determination to build a successful life and career for herself. I read *Educated* by Tara Westover, about her childhood in a paranoid survivalist family and her pursuit to educate herself. I read *Men We Reaped* by Jesmyn Ward, her story about the heartbreaking losses of the five close men in her life over a period of four years to drugs, suicide and accidents and living with the heart-wrenching grief that followed.

Their stories of grit lit a small fire of hope inside of me. I read furiously for the first time in my life. The more I read about them, the more I wanted to read about them. And as soon as I put down one of these memoirs, I would begin to search online for the author's images and all available videos.

I wanted to see what courage looked like.

I would find myself staring intently at each of their faces, scrutinising their features in detail. I would replay their interviews, over and over again, closely observing their articulation, hand gestures and postures.

Courage, from what I could see, was uniquely beautiful in all its glory.

They were African American women with deep caramel skin tones and tightly curled hair. They were Caucasian women with blonde, straight hair and striking blue or green eyes. They were women of different racial backgrounds who lived through different eras of time and faced a range of tragedies. Yet, there was something indistinguishable about each one of them—it was the unmistakable sparkle of resilience, of hope in their eyes.

Soon, something magical began to happen. I slowly started to see myself in them. Their stories were wildly different from mine and, sometimes, far more traumatic, yet I found hints of my not-so-normal life in theirs. In their narratives, I saw my own anguish, my own struggle, but also my own stubbornness to survive.

A profound realisation dawned on me—my fear of turning into my mother was absolutely irrational. I realised that although we bore a striking physical resemblance to each other, with our short slender physique, wrinkled necks and jet-black hair which greyed out pre-maturely in our 20s, that's where the similarities ended.

In every other aspect, I couldn't have been more unlike her. I understood that her trauma was relentless and punishing and there were parts of it that completely justified her insanity; but from that moment on, I also knew that I was not her, that we were two very different women.

I was more like those women in the gallery of Google Images who were complete strangers to me; who didn't share an iota of my genetic makeup, but whose hearts had once burnt with the same fire that burnt inside my heart today.

Through all their stories, ran a common thread. It was the distant yet visible silver living in the future amidst the dark clouds of the present. It was their stubborn belief that this couldn't possibly be the end, that there existed a vastly different end that patiently awaited them. It was the intrinsic nature that has been core to human survival through countless calamities, genocides, famines and wars—it was hope. It was hope, against hope, of a future that was worth enduring the miserable present for.

I knew what I needed.

All I needed was a conduit of hope to hold on to, even if for the time being; something real or imaginary, tangible or intangible, a truth or a lie.

I was a parched, dying man, gasping with my last breaths, lying defeated in the heat of an arid desert. Suddenly, by a miracle of sorts, I had spotted a water body. It could be a water body, it could be a mirage. What it was didn't matter at all. What mattered was that it was something that had suddenly charged me with the vitality to start running towards it.

***

My hope for the future, my meaning, my purpose didn't materialise out of thin air as soon as I embarked on my quest for it. Alas, I wasn't deeply passionate about anything in my life—no skill, no cause, no God, nothing at all.

There were definitely some fragments of yearnings, scattered here and there, of things and feelings that interested me, that on gloomy days had brought a smile to my face, that I had hoped for in fleeting moments of my everyday life. However, I couldn't really put a pin on any of them to declare in all earnestness, "Boom, this is the purpose of my life!"

So, I decided to start with whatever little I had. I began by piecing together those fragments and shaping up a version 2.0 of the "Get Back to Life Plan." However, this time around, I simply called it a "Life Plan." I realised that by creating the "Get Back to Life Plan," I was attempting to reclaim the life that I would have had if my husband was still alive, if the events that I had lived through hadn't transpired at all. That plan was inherently flawed and was set for failure at the very outset.

This time around, the plan wasn't just for a year either. I realised it was too aspirational. It was mapped until I would turn fifty. Sixteen full, good years. I figured that was ample time to rewrite my story.

My "Life Plan" was bucketed in four areas that I finalised after a lot of internal deliberation.

1. Love and Belonging

2. Exploring the World

3. Personal Growth

4. Professional and Financial Growth

38

Love and Belonging

1. Love and Belonging

Belonging was the first piece of the puzzle to solve, for it was the absolute loss of belonging that had stirred up the emotional upheaval in me. Tucked between Abhinav's arms, with my head resting on his chest, I had found home for the very first time. I had, for once, belonged to someone truly and deeply. But now, there was not a single place, person or feeling that I belonged to anymore.

The real question, however, remained—did I really wish to belong, since all that belonging had ever brought me was endless suffering?

For as long as I could remember, I had grappled with a never-ending internal conflict—detachment vs belonging—the tussle which had intensified over time. There were parts of me that wanted both, but what was it that I wanted more?

On one hand, there was science and research, which was unequivocally shouting in support of belonging. I read through countless research projects conducted over decades, each concluding independently that: real happiness was a result of meaningful relationships nurtured over time, with friends, family and communities. People who were socially connected tended to live longer, healthier lives. And so on and so forth.

All the research felt utterly unfair towards people like me who couldn't even keep the people around them alive. Then how the hell were we supposed to form lasting, meaningful relations? How were *we* supposed to find a sense of belonging?

On the other hand, my tryst with destiny so far had made it abundantly clear that detachment from the world was the key to freeing myself of misery. It was natural for me to gravitate towards detachment, especially when it seemed like I was up against the entire world, lonelier than ever in my grief. It was easier to detach from my extended family, considering they were hundreds of kilometres away from me. It was easier to detach from my mother and my brother, when that is how we had learned to deal with tragedy in our lives—letting each other rot in our own miseries.

But the same was proving particularly difficult to achieve with Abhinav's parents; their language of love was entirely different from what I had known all my life. They insisted on calling me every day, they nudged me for frequent visits to their place and they would occasionally drop by unexpectedly to check on me. All this felt a little too smothering, a little too intrusive.

So I retaliated and attempted to push them away. I was adamant in the pursuit of becoming my best hyper-independent self because nobody could be trusted anymore, nobody could be depended on. I needed to be in complete control of my life because that was how I could break the cycle of loss and grief.

But they still persisted, and I was unable to figure out why.

It was the first Diwali after Abhinav's death, and I couldn't bear the sight of any of it. The bustling markets, the glittering decorations, the festive cheer all around, reminded me of everything I had lost.

I couldn't stand being around it, so I decided to work remotely from Goa for an entire month. As I hopped from one Airbnb to another, from the north to the south of Goa, I hoped that the cool breeze of the sea would rub-off some of Goa's *Susegad (Konkani word for quiet, peace and contentment)* way of life on me and bring me tranquillity. Sadly, the opposite happened. I ended up being more miserable than I was at home.

While I was returning from Goa, Papa kept insisting on meeting me at the airport. We had not seen each other for over a month. But I stubbornly refused, mostly out of spite.

"I just want to spend a few hours with you," he insisted. "I will drive you to your home, we will have a quick cup of tea together and I will leave. Nothing more." I continued to decline his offer. I didn't want to see him or anyone else; I wanted to rot in my misery alone.

On the day of my flight, as I walked out of the Delhi airport, I saw him there, patiently waiting at the Arrivals gate. It was a mildly chilly evening, at the onset of winter, and he stood there in his brown woollen Nehru jacket.

As he spotted me in the crowd, his face lit up in a broad smile that squinted his eyes in a way that reminded me of Abhinav. He had brought along a half litre milk pouch and tiny containers filled with tea leaves and sugar. We quietly drove to Gurgaon and shared that cup of tea. And then, just as he had promised, he returned to Delhi.

It was then that I understood that Mom and Papa weren't going anywhere.

Papa helped me navigate through Abhinav's official paperwork, settling his bank accounts, selling off his car and sorting out his belongings. He also took on the task of giving me driving lessons, something I had been nagging Abhinav about for ages.

Although I vehemently refused all help from him, deep down, I was secretly glad that he and Mom were there by my side. I wanted to push them away; I wanted to detach. But one day, I just couldn't do that anymore. It had started to become exhausting. I began to realise that I will have to live with the terrifying, yet reassuring feeling that belonging was.

How could I not belong when belonging is all that I had ever wanted?

But, I needed to recognise and rectify the fallacy of my attachment to Abhinav—how I had anchored all my sense of belonging exclusively to him. How unfair I had been, burdening him with the expectations of every conceivable relationship that a person could possibly have. Along with being my husband, I had also expected him to be my best friend, my sibling, my mom, my dad, my career counsellor, my everything.

Perhaps the only way that I could solve this puzzle—to belong but also detach—was by scattering all the "belonging" that I had once housed in Abhinav among all the people whose lives were intertwined with mine in some way or the other.

1. My brother: We suffer in silence, separated by a distance of hundreds of kilometres, both alone and together in our history of suffering. I belonged to him.

2. My mother: Suffering, some mine, some hers, was what had distanced us from each other. But if not in any other sense, then in that rudimentary biological sense in which all animal offsprings belong to their mother, I belonged to her. I might resent her, I might not want to be her, but, I did belong to her.

3. Abhinav's parents: We suffer together from the same suffering and it is in this suffering that I belong to them.

4. My cousins: Suffering was the sharp, piercing thread tightly wrapped around our bodies, inflicting deep wounds on every inch that it touched. Yet, it was also the very thread that continued to fiercely bind us together. We held hands and wailed as the men of our family fell, one after the other. We were young adults, some much younger than others, thrust into adulthood without the guiding light of fathers. In the absence of those fathers, we each made our mistakes, we each weaved a path different from others. Some stayed together, while others drifted away. A part of me would always belong to them and the joyous and precarious past I shared with them.

Suffering is what binds me to all of them, suffering is what binds us the strongest. In the moment that we shed our inhibitions of social compliance; in the moment when we let the injured primal human run amok with anger, frustration and tears; it is then, in that moment of vulnerability, we forge a bond that is unbreakable, that is inescapable.

In my "Life Plan," I slotted a crucial entry for December 2022: "Mend my relationships with them all." Using my grief as an excuse, I had deliberately detached myself from many of those relations.

Following that, I added a new entry under the *Love and Belonging* section to my plan for 2023: "Adopt a puppy." I had never had a pet before, but I had always longed for one. I wanted to feel the unconditional love of a furry friend; waking up to snuggles and the lively commotion of an enthusiastic pup in my home sounded like a dream. I pictured this pet as a female Cocker Spaniel and had already picked a name for her: Mindy, as an homage to Mindy Kaling, whose TV show was a huge solace during many challenging and lonely nights.

This was followed by some more wishful thinking as I scribbled "Adopt a child" somewhere in 2026. I knew it was a lofty goal and it would be undoubtedly challenging to raise a child alone. Yet, I had to put it there.

I dreamed of having a little girl joyfully prancing around the house in an adorable tulle dress. I wanted to make the prettiest pigtails for her and tie them in beautiful, bright ribbons. I wanted to see the world anew through her innocent eyes, to introduce her to the warmth of the sun, the splattering touch of rain, the vastness of the sea. I wanted to watch her as she discovered the world, one bit at a time, her eyes filled with boundless wonder and amazement. I wanted to love and protect her with an unwavering fierceness, but also with an equal nonchalance to give her the room to blossom into her own being.

39

Other Buckets

2. Exploring the World

Ilive through you, just as you live through me, and somehow we manage to live through this together.

When it came to our preferences for holiday locations, Abhinav and I couldn't have been more dissimilar. My idea of a perfect getaway was always a few days of leisure at a luxurious tropical resort, where I could lounge by the pool, engrossed in a good book, savouring frozen margaritas. Abhinav's heart, on the contrary, was set in the wild. He wanted to go on arduous treks, conquer formidable mountain peaks and dive into deep oceans—and he wanted me to be his partner in all those adventures.

I would decline outright. To me, the idea of taking time out of my draining job and subjecting myself to such discomfort just for the sake of an adrenaline rush seemed ludicrous. To my refusal, he would often remark, "You don't know yet, but once you have cherished sleeping under the starry skies on a mountain, there is nothing else you would want more."

Strangely enough, my first ever trip following Abhinav's death was a high altitude trek in the Lahaul Spiti region of Himachal Pradesh. It was as if he was calling me there. I could feel his presence everywhere. He was in the serenity of the breathtaking landscape and the grandeur of the tall pines, he was in the innocence of the wrinkled smiles of the locals and the music of the hidden springs. All of it reminded me of him.

As a first for me, I ended up spending a night in a tent out in the open.

When sleep eluded me in the stillness of the night, I stepped outside and stood there in the vast expanse of nothing but nature. For several minutes at a stretch, I stared intently at the glorious sky beaded with millions of stars. My breath laboured owing to low oxygen at 18,000 feet, my hands cold with the harsh winds and my heart full of regret for the memories that didn't get created.

How I wished, then, for a chance to have accompanied Abhinav on one of his adventures. How I wished to have shared that remarkable moment with him, to tell him, "You were right all along! It is, indeed, beautiful."

Travel was, in fact, a window into one of the most incredible aspects of Abhinav's life. Perusing through the photographs from his world travels, I would often imagine the nervous excitement of the twenty-something Abhinav as he had embarked on that journey of nine months.

The more I looked at those pictures, the more it felt as if those places were summoning me. A fresh wave of exhilaration had seized me. I wanted to explore the historical cities in Europe and feast my eyes on the breathtaking architecture. I wanted to plunge into the depths of Southeast Asian seas and witness the grand marine life. I wanted to drive across the scenic views of New Zealand with the wind flowing through my hair.

I wanted to visit every single one of those locations, to immerse myself in all those experiences that Abhinav had lived through. I wanted to trace back his footsteps and perhaps even meet all the people that he had crossed paths with during his travels.

So what if Abhinav didn't leave me endearing letters to guide me through my life after he was gone? Perhaps he left behind those hard drives and the pictures in them as a sign, as his way of nudging me to lead a life of adventure similar to his. Perhaps that is how I could live through him, and he through me, and we could both survive the passage of all the time that was to come.

When you are desperate for meaning, meaning becomes ubiquitous and everything around you begins to manifest into that meaning. When your soul is stubborn for survival, it will grab every little thing it can find as food to nourish that famished spirit.

So, in this next bucket on my "Life Plan," I began to slot travel to all the countries and locations that Abhinav had visited.

3. Personal Growth

Among my small yearnings were also things of interest that I had been putting off for years—Kathak, swimming, learning to play an instrument—things that had faded in the background of life's constant hustle.

In fact, Kathak as an art is something I had always cherished and had attended classes sporadically over the years. Every once in a while, I have found myself browsing through videos of the dance form, admiring the artists and longing to dance with the same expressions, coordination and unwavering focus as them.

I remembered the early days of my relationship with Abhinav, when I had tried to impress him with a slightly fabricated piece of information about my accomplishments outside of work. "I am trained in Kathak," I had claimed.

When the truth was finally exposed, Abhinav would often jokingly exclaim, "I have been catfished! You told me you are a trained dancer, but I have never seen you perform. Need to get a refund from pandit ji who officiated our marriage."

I slotted to learn those skills over the coming years.

4. Professional and Financial Growth

Professional growth and financial stability were equally important. Just because life had been hard and I was on a journey to self-discovery didn't mean I should have to abandon all that I had built over a decade of my career. To find my life's purpose, I shouldn't have to become a monk and give up my (metaphorical) Ferrari and every other worldly possession; the two didn't have to be necessarily mutually exclusive. And, of course, in a more pragmatic sense, I needed my career and the income that it generated to fund all the other buckets of my "Life Plan."

So, I slotted for milestones of career and financial growth in the plan.

After I had meticulously catalogued all the items I could think of within the four buckets, there were still a few thoughts that lingered in my mind, but I couldn't really find a house for them in any of the existing buckets. They seemed trivial yet crucial, so I decided to introduce a fifth bucket and named it "Things of Joy." Anyway, five buckets had a better ring to it than four.

5. Things of Joy

It was a catch-all bucket for all my random whims and fancies that I would daydream about—oftentimes sitting idly at home or in the middle of a busy day at work. Although there was no specific timeline associated with any of them, I wanted to note them down to not lose sight of them.

They were perhaps the expression of my renewed desire to indulge in the beauty of life; born out of my recent urge to remind myself of what it meant to be human, and more importantly, what it meant to be alive.

Under the bucket, I noted anything and everything that felt even remotely romantic about life and living. "Dance in the rain," I scribbled; I couldn't remember the last time I did that. "Experience snow," I added.

I went on to add trivial experiences that had brought me even the slightest of joy recently: "Go to your favourite café to have your favourite cappuccino every week," "Pet a dog," "Talk to a toddler."

***

The "Life Plan" was ready, and with its completion came a renewed sense of hope. The plan was the confluence point of all my hopes and aspirations, small and big, which alone and scattered didn't mean anything, but together they defined my meaning, my purpose, my silver lining.

It may not have been as extraordinary as I had initially sought it out to be, but it seemed efficacious. The Plan became a small window into my future thoughtfully crafted on a spreadsheet. A future that was markedly different from the one I had imagined a year back, but nevertheless, a future worth living for.

"It is a peculiarity of man that he can only live by looking to the future," Viktor Frankl has written in *Man's Search for Meaning*.

On days when life appeared bleak again, when it felt as if there was no point in continuing like this, I would open up the spreadsheet. I would take time to glance through the different sections and the goals and hopes I had added in each of them. Seeing it all together in one place would make my eyes sparkle, because I knew I was going to survive.

There was hope for me as well. There was a lot to live for.

There was, however, one crucial catch. For the "Life Plan" to really work this time, I had to accept the fact that change is the only constant. That it would be alright if I was unable to achieve the timelines as per the plan, it would be alright if the plan continued to evolve, and it would be completely alright if I veered away from my initial beliefs about what mattered and what didn't.

In order to break free from the cycle of misery caused by the mountain of expectations from life, I had to be more accepting of the "Life Plan" being a continuously evolving document—a document that would iterate from version v1.0 to v2.0 to v3.0 and possibly all the way to version v1000.0, with some deliberate and other destined changes, as a consequence of how my life would unravel through the days, months, years and decades to come.

40

About Survival and Acceptance

Time does heal, as they say, but not as absolutely as they might think.

Time today, as a construct, has lost all its meaning. Sometimes it feels like an eternity since I last had Abhinav by my side, and other times, it feels like it was only yesterday that we celebrated our first wedding anniversary. Strangely enough, sometimes it also feels like we were never really together, as though it was a beautiful dream that I have been violently shaken up from to live a life that was always this lonely. However, never does it feel like it has been a year and a half.

Time, instead, is now neatly divided into two epochs—Before Abhinav and After Abhinav.

In the middle of a workday, as I sift through my inbox looking for an old email or search for a dated WhatsApp message on my phone, I find my eyes intuitively trying to locate the date of the communication. Each time, the very first thought that crosses my mind as I spot the date is, "Was Abinav alive at that time? Had I met him by that time? Where were we on that day?" As a reflex, my mind immediately travels to that day in the past. *September 10, 2018: Leaving for the US after spending three amazing months with him. August 20, 2019: Getting introduced to his parents. February 20, 2020: Nervous butterflies in the stomach just a few days before the wedding. May 10, 2021: The beginning of the end.*

My mind wanders, spaced out in the past, completely forgetting about the task at hand. It strolls for a good amount of time before coming back to reality. The mood for the rest of the day ranges from ecstatic to anxious based on the date of the message that has been unearthed.

I still sleep on my side of the bed, the left side. It is not by conscious choice, but my body somehow doesn't feel comfortable in the middle, nor does it drift unconsciously to his side.

On worse days, I wake up in the middle of the night, breaking into a cold, shivering sweat. I have seen Abhinav again in the ICU bed, gasping for air in his purple gown. I see myself pushing through the crowd of doctors and nurses, desperate to keep holding onto his hand.

On better days, I wake up imagining him sitting on his side of the bed, attempting to catch up on his sleep, as he always did early in the morning. I stretch out my arm, with my eyes still closed, to stroke his back to signal to him that it is quite early. I tell him in whispers, "If you are still sleepy, why don't you lie down for another thirty minutes?" I am fully awakened in despair at the rude reminder of his absence as I find my hand reaching into thin air.

The otherness I feel from the world has grown more profound; I am an outsider again. I observe people in malls, on roads, in offices, in cafes. I study their expressions from a distance; their ceaseless chatter, their haste to be somewhere, their hand gestures, their movements. I don't identify with any of it anymore. I have been pushed outside the ever beckoning toy store again; I certainly do not belong. This time around, I don't *wish* to belong. It doesn't bother me anymore; normalcy is not a goal anymore.

But embracing the "abnormal" doesn't come naturally to me either. On some days, to be deliriously happy for a fleeting moment, I conjure up Abhinav and fantasise about our lives together. I nudge my mind to travel to this parallel universe where he is still alive and within my reach. I imagine being together at our home, which is filled with the aroma of a new recipe in the making and the sounds of constant laughter.

Sadly, this parallel universe isn't vigorous enough to take full control of me, and I am somehow still left with the awareness of the present. I continue to fight my reality, trying to perpetuate this illusion for that fleeting boost of dopamine.

There are days when I find myself genuinely enjoying time with friends, blissfully laughing while savouring my favourite coffee. Moments filled with joyous breeziness. And then, out of nowhere, flashbacks hit me, and just like that I am consumed by a sinking feeling in my gut.

Sometimes it is my mother's face, blood gushing out of her nose. Other times it is my dad's face, his eyes red and cloudy as he wails endlessly for help. Yet other times it is Abhinav's face, as he slips into death and turns away from me.

At times, it's just me, alone, sitting on a cold iron bench in a hospital waiting room. I'm wearing the green kurta with the pink flowers that I wore almost every day while Abhinav was in the hospital; it is torn at the hem from getting caught somewhere.

I see the room lit with harsh lights in the middle of the night. I notice my legs shaking and my hands folded in prayer. But I am unable to discern whether it is my husband or my father or someone else who is admitted there.

I see a doctor approaching me. He asks, "Is there someone else whom we can talk to?"

Cut to the present, I am no longer paying attention to the ongoing conversation. Instead I am asking myself, "Is there someone else? Will there ever be someone else?" I am furious and helpless all over again. My heart is thumping so vigorously that I fear that it would startle the entire room.

The bliss that I experience is ephemeral, the pain I carry is permanent.

I don't resist those flashbacks anymore, which now live permanently in the depths of my memory, clearer than all the other memories that I have ever created. I don't deny them their right to my soul. I allow them to flow; I allow them to take control of me. I let them remind me of who I am.

Coming back to the question that continues to loom, "Who am I? What is my story about?"

It was the beginning of July, and Gurgaon was nearing the onset of monsoons. I was working from home late one evening when I heard the thundering of clouds. It was going to pour heavily. I decided to pause whatever I was doing and step out as the showers began to hit the dry cemented roads of my colony.

Shame, so deeply ingrained in me, seized me as soon as I started to walk in the rain. I felt exposed. Shame was nudging me to walk briskly, to act as if I was not doing this purposely; that I was not there savouring the rain but instead rushing somewhere to protect myself from it.

Feeling absolutely, completely free doesn't come easy.

I noticed people had started to come out on their balconies to watch the rain. I could feel some of their gazes on me. So I walked faster and further away from my apartment. The downpour was so torrential that in just a few minutes my entire body was fully drenched. I stopped where I was and decided not to run anymore.

With a lot of hesitation, I slowly opened my arms wide and tilted my face up to let go of the shame—the shame of who I was and the shame of what had happened. I refuse to carry it henceforth, it is not mine to carry or hide.

It is the shame of the gods above.

I stood there, soaking in the rain and in a newfound tingling feeling, for what seemed like an eternity, but might have been just ten minutes.

As I walked back toward my apartment all by myself, the street lights shone from behind me as if they were deliberately set there to throw a spotlight on me. I walked slowly, my body not stiff with angst anymore, but loosened with pride, as I freed myself from everything that had clenched me for ages.

I had finally taken centre stage; I was the main character of my movie.

This seemingly normal evening felt like a critical juncture in my life—a moment of acceptance of who I was, a moment of acceptance of my history. A moment of triumph. A moment of clarity about my story.

A moment of realisation that my story was indeed about basic human survival; about how millions of us pick ourselves up, quietly, from big and small adversities every day; carrying a hope in our heart that one day things will be different.

It is one hell of a story to live for.

As soon as I came back, even before changing into dry clothes, I opened the "Life Plan" on my laptop and marked "Dance in the rain" as complete. I didn't literally dance, but we can leave the technicalities out of it.

I woke up with a stuffy nose and a fever the next morning, but it was all worth it.

I had survived.

***

About survival—if you have access to decent nutrition to nourish your body, a hope to nourish your soul and just a few people to keep nudging you to live, you will not perish. That is all that is needed to survive, nothing more, but also nothing less.

We do not give enough credit to the wonderful anatomy of our bodies, the peculiar mechanism that has evolved to help us survive against all odds. I didn't eat a morsel for days, I didn't move for months, I cried endlessly day and night. I was ridden by a constant debilitating pain in my chest. I was convinced that my body would give up eventually.

But the human body, built on the very foundation of evolution over thousands of years, is persistent like nothing else. Its ability to thrive in the most punishing of life situations is astonishing. Even when others give up on you, even when your soul gives up, it is your body that will be there, standing alone, waving from the stands, cheering for you.

About acceptance—it is the acceptance of our realities that will set us free from the envy, the anger, the despair that stems from the inequity of misery. But acceptance doesn't come easy. It has taken a lot to accept...

That Abhinav is not coming back.

That my mother will probably never be a mother to me.

That I will never get the answer to why me or why Abhinav.

That I will never be the same kind of happy again.

That my life will perhaps never be normal in the traditional sense, but it will be a different kind of normal, it will be my very own kind of normal.

I am thirty-four as I pen the last chapters of this book, and anxiety grips me again. I wonder if it is too soon to conclude this story. I fear what is yet to come, I fear the tragedies that I am yet to live through. I fear that one of them might eventually break me.

But, then, there is also a little part of me that is hopeful, or maybe incurably delusional. Despite the awareness of the randomness of it all, that part still thrives on the belief that the balance between suffering and bliss would ultimately be restored, that there is hope for redemption from pain and misery within this lifetime.

How wonderful it would have been if life was not so uncertain, and if there was a scale of suffering that defined the upper limit of how bad it can get. A scale which all of us could refer to, to say how far we were from salvation from our pain. But there isn't—if you believe you have suffered enough doesn't mean you won't suffer anymore. It also doesn't mean that you will always suffer.

Perhaps the only real solace in life, ironically, lies in the same aspect of it that we fear the most—*its uncertainty*; that there is no finality as we continue to live, neither in bliss but also not in suffering.